INVITATION TO THE OLD TESTAMENT

By the Same Author

Hosea-Jonah (The Layman's Bible Commentary)
I Chronicles (The Anchor Bible)
II Chronicles (The Anchor Bible)
Ezra and Nehemiah (The Anchor Bible)
The Linguistic and Literary Form of the Book of Ruth

Invitation to the Old Testament

JACOB M. MYERS

1966

DOUBLEDAY & COMPANY, INC.

Garden City, New York

To
My grandchildren
Robert, Barbara and Mary Ann

PREFACE

This little book is intended to whet the appetite of the reader to explore for himself the immense treasures deposited in the Old Testament. Much material, including a number of books, has been omitted to keep it short for easier reading. Others might have selected different subjects and biblical illustrations, but the ones utilized appear to the writer to reflect basic themes.

It was written primarily for the ordinary layman who may be desirous of knowing what this often neglected portion of our Bible has to say for itself and to discover what relevance it may have for this or any other age, and, more specifically, what it may have to offer by way of guidance and direction in dealing with the plethora of personal, social, and religious problems prevalent today. What appears here represents some of the buoyant lessons learned in the course of more than thirty-five years preaching and more than a quarter century of teaching in a seminary.

The name of the Hebrew deity, Yahweh, is used interchangeably with Lord. The Scripture translations from the Old Testament are the writer's; those from the New Testament follow, for the most part, the Revised Standard Version.

The first twenty-six chapters were originally written for *The Lutheran* magazine. Most of them have been considerably expanded here. Gratitude for permission to reprint them in book

form is hereby expressed to the editor, Dr. G. Elson Ruff. To list
the names of all those from whom I have learned and borrowed,
perhaps substantially at times, would be impossible. But I do
record herewith my deepest appreciation to all of them. I owe
a special debt of gratitude to my patient wife and to my devoted
typist for her excellent work in interpreting almost illegible
manuscripts.

J. M. Myers
Gettysburg, Pennsylvania

CONTENTS

I	Why the Old Testament?	1
II	In the Beginning God (Genesis 1–11)	9
III	Abraham Our Father (Genesis 12–50)	23
IV	Out of Egypt I Called My Son (Exodus 1–19)	31
V	I Am the Lord Thy God (Exodus 20)	37
VI	Sacrifices and Offerings (Leviticus 1–16)	43
VII	The Way of the Wilderness (Numbers)	49
VIII	A Land Flowing with Milk and Honey (Joshua)	55
IX	Struggle for a Homeland (Judges)	61
X	We Want a King! (I Samuel)	67
XI	The Son of Jesse (I Samuel 16–II Samuel 24)	73
XII	Courting Disaster (I Kings 1–11)	79
XIII	The End of the Beginning (I Kings 12:1–24, 14:21–31)	85
XIV	A Champion for the Lord (I Kings 17–21, II Kings 1)	91
XV	A Niagara of Righteousness (Amos)	97
XVI	Covenant Love (Hosea)	103
XVII	A Holy God (Isaiah 1–39)	109
XVIII	O Bethlehem Ephrathah (Micah)	115
XIX	A New Covenant (Jeremiah)	121

XX	A New Community (Ezekiel 40–48)	127
XXI	Prophets and Prophets (Zephaniah, Nahum, Habakkuk)	135
XXII	Speaking to the Heart of Jerusalem (Isaiah 40–66)	141
XXIII	Prophets of a New Israel (Haggai and Zechariah)	151
XXIV	Gifts of Wisdom (Proverbs)	157
XXV	The Man from Uz (Job)	165
XXVI	The Notebook of a Skeptic (Ecclesiastes)	173
XXVII	The Hymnbook of Israel (Psalms)	181
XXVIII	The Way of Love (Canticles)	191
XXIX	A New Beginning (Chronicles, Ezra, Nehemiah)	199
XXX	Denouement (Daniel)	211
XXXI	In Conclusion	221
	Bibliography	229
	Indexes	239

INVITATION TO THE OLD TESTAMENT

WHY THE OLD TESTAMENT?

Such a question would, in all probability, not occur to the average Christian. He takes it more or less for granted that the Old Testament is a portion of his Bible, perhaps a little more bulky than convenient but nevertheless of some importance just because it occupies the place it does. Listening to the sermons of his pastor year after year, he might wonder—just out of curiosity—of what use the excess baggage could be. It must puzzle him a bit why the Old Testament comes ahead of the New in his book since his pastor uses it so infrequently and sometimes appears to hint that, inasmuch as we now have the New Testament, we no longer need the Old. After all, does not the Bible itself speak of the Lord's doing "a new thing," of making "all things new"? So we now have the "new"; the "old" is passé—good in its time and while it lasted but now obsolete.

The Old Testament Is Holy Scripture

With just a bit of probing, it becomes abundantly evident that a superficial handling of the Old Testament is inexcusable. It cannot be shrugged off as outmoded or superseded by the advent of Jesus Christ and therefore dispensable. It remains Holy Scripture for Christianity and Judaism, and is of importance also to Islam. The Talmud, which is commentary, interpretation and direction for Jewish living, has but one aim—to apply the

Torah, in its widest sense, to the resolution of the problems of life in every contingency and thus bring the community into obedience to the commandments of God. Whether Muhammad's knowledge of the Bible came from Jewish communities in Arabia or from contact with Christians, the impact of the Old Testament upon the Qur'an is unmistakable.

For example, the basic doctrine of the Old Testament is that of the unity of God. "Hear, O Israel, Yahweh our God is one Yahweh" (Deut. 6:4) might be compared with, "Say, God is one God, the eternal God. He neither begets, nor is begotten and there is none like him" (Surah 112). It has been observed that in the Qur'an the names of Adam, Noah and Abraham occur about seventy times each. That of Moses is found in thirty-four of the one hundred and fourteen Surahs. Frequently mentioned are Ishmael, Lot, Jacob, Joseph, Saul, David, Solomon, Job, Elijah and Jonah. The story of creation and the fall are referred to five times, the story of the flood and Sodom about eight times. The Old Testament is used in the Qur'an somewhat in the same fashion as it is in the Mishnah and the New Testament. George Sale says, "Mohammed acknowledged the divine authority of the Pentateuch, Psalms and Gospel."*

For the Christian the Old Testament is more than promise, or prediction of the coming Redeemer. It is Word of God itself. It is not simply background material for the New Testament or the repository of historical incidents transmitted to satisfy the curiosity of later generations. Indeed, there is a sense in which the Old Testament is Word of God par excellence. Therein is

* The Koran (Philadelphia, 1853), p. 54 of the Preliminary Discourse.

disclosed and demonstrated the creative and sustaining activity of God, his mighty acts of salvation and judgment. No alert reader can fail to be instructed and inspired by the down-to-earth qualities of the relationship between God and man depicted on every page. There is no vague theologizing. God just is. He acts in and through the experiences of his people. He tells them how things are in their world, shows them the operative structure of the moral universe, chastises them with prophets when they are in violation of the covenant, warns them of impending doom when they persist in their foibles and follies and, though they ignore his pleas, he never ceases to love them. Our Lord has epitomized the long, checkered history of Israel—"How often would I . . . but you would not" (Matt. 23:37).

The Old Testament Was the Bible of Jesus

The Old Testament was Holy Scripture for Jesus and the apostles. The Master-Teacher grounded all his life and work upon it and in it. By it he resisted the onslaughts of the Satan. With "It is written, 'Man does not live by bread alone, but by every word that proceeds from the mouth of God'" (Matt. 4:4—a quotation from Deut. 8:3), he responded to the Satan who bade him turn stones into bread. When tempted to cast himself down from the pinnacle of the Temple, Jesus replied, "You must not tempt the Lord your God" (Matt. 4:7—a quotation from Deut. 6:16). Exhorted to worship the Satan to gain possession and control of the kingdoms of the world with their glory, he observed, "You must worship the Lord your God and serve him alone" (Matt. 4:10—a quotation from Deut. 6:13). "Have you not read what David did when he was hungry, also those with him" (Matt. 12:3—a reference to I Sam. 21:1-6; Lev. 24:9); "have you not read that he who made them at the beginning made them male and female" (Matt. 19:4—the reference is to Gen. 1:27).

Jesus often chided his people for misinterpreting the Old Testament word—"You know neither the scriptures nor the power of God" (Matt. 22:29), or for the failure to take it seriously—"What is written in the law? How do you read?" (Luke 10:26). Upon it he laid the foundation of his mission, as we read in Luke 4:16–21:

> And he came to Nazareth, where he was brought up; and he went into the synagogue, as his custom was, on the sabbath day. And he stood up to read; and there was given to him the book of the prophet Isaiah. He opened the book and found the place where it was written, "The Spirit of the Lord is upon me, because he has anointed me to preach good news to the poor. He has sent me to proclaim release to the captives and recovery of sight to the blind, to set at liberty those who are oppressed, to proclaim the acceptable year of the Lord." . . . And he began to say to them, "Today this scripture has been fulfilled in your hearing."

In the parable of the rich man and Lazarus he further stressed the validity and essentiality of the scriptures of his people:

> They have Moses and the prophets; let them hear them. . . . If they hear not Moses and the prophets, neither will they be convinced if some one should rise from the dead.
>
> (Luke 16:29, 31)

He drew personal comfort from the Hebrew Bible in the most distressing and agonizing moments of his life: ". . . It is written, 'I will strike the shepherd, and the sheep will be scattered' " (Mark 14:27—a quotation from Zech. 13:7). "My God, my God, why have you forsaken me?" (Mark 15:34—a quotation from Ps. 22:1). He called upon its testimony again and again to attest his direction to those around him.

The apostolic conception of the Old Testament may be judged from frequent references to it as the source for the pattern of life and thought followed by the Master. To the Thessalonian Jews Paul quoted "texts of Scripture" (Acts 17:2), Apollos "demonstrated from the scriptures that the Messiah was Jesus" (Acts 18:28), Peter linked the events connected with the passion of Christ to the witness of the scriptures (Acts 1:15–22; 2:14–36), and Philip interpreted a portion of Isaiah 53 to the Ethiopian eunuch (Acts 8:26–35). It is quite evident that every Christian community, without exception, was founded on the Old Testament as its basic and *only* Scripture. The New Testament had not yet come into being.

Looking at the New Testament itself it is clear that the framers of its gospel documents followed literary patterns established by Old Testament writers. The Gospel of Mark is, according to some scholars, modeled on the Elijah stories of I Kings. Certainly Matthew had in mind the divine address from Sinai when he reported the Sermon on the Mount and the five divisions of his work correspond to the five books of Moses. The great psalms of Luke's Gospel (Magnificat, Benedictus and Nunc Dimittis) resemble the immortal Psalms of the Old Testament. Even the parabolic method of teaching so effectively used by Jesus originated in the proverbial literature of the Old Scripture.

The Old Testament in the New

The careful reader of the New Testament must have observed the many cross references to almost all books of the Bible. While statistics almost never tell the whole story, in this case it is interesting to note that the Revised Standard Version in its footnotes cites more than thirteen hundred Old Testament passages which are either direct quotations or allusions. The lists in Henry Barclay Swete's *Introduction to the Old Testament in Greek* ([Cambridge, 1900], pp. 382–91) and the appendix to Nestle's *Novum Testamentum Graece* ([Stuttgart, 1950], pp. 658–71) offer a graphic picture of the situation. Swete lists the specific passages quoted in each of the books of the New Testament as follows: Matthew has forty, Mark nineteen, Luke seventeen, John twelve, Acts twenty-three, the Epistles of John none and the so-called Catholic Epistles few. Romans has forty-two, I and II Corinthians nineteen, Galatians ten. Of the imprisonment letters (Colossians, Philippians, Ephesians, Philemon) only Ephesians has five direct quotations. Hebrews quotes twenty-eight passages. The author of Revelation does not quote at all directly, though his work is full of Old Testament phrases and allusions. It must be remembered that Swete's data are based, not on the Hebrew Bible, but on the Septuagint (the Greek Bible), where Hebrew references are frequently obscured. The Nestle appendix lists all quotations or allusions with reference to each book of the Old Testament (thirteen and a half double-columned pages); in this text of the New Testament direct quotations are indicated with boldface type. Edward Reuss, more than a hundred years ago (1862), wrote: "There is hardly a page in the New Testament where the Old is not cited."*

Of paramount importance, however, is the ideological milieu in which the New Testament moves. It is basically a Hebrew book as may be seen from a simple catalogue of terminology—word, truth, glory, peace, covenant, spirit, life, day of the Lord,

* *History of the Canon*, trans. from the 2d French ed. by David Hunter (New York, 1884), p. 5.

sin, suffering, servant, salvation, and many others. Those fundamental terms so fraught with meaning simply cannot be understood without a thorough knowledge of the original framework in which they occur.

Conclusion

The above observations are reason enough for the reading of the Old Testament but perhaps the best argument of all for it is the fact that the New Testament cannot possibly stand alone. It requires the weight of the more than fifteen hundred years of Hebrew religio-historical experience to prevent its evaporation in speculative theology or erosion of the incarnational aspects of God's revelation by a subtle gnostic attitude toward history.

Finally, in the words of Sir George Adam Smith, "What was indispensable to the Redeemer must always be indispensable to the redeemed."*

* *Modern Criticism and the Preaching of the Old Testament*, 2d ed. (New York, 1901), p. 11.

II

IN THE BEGINNING GOD

(Genesis 1–11)

The early traditions of the Hebrew people begin, continue and end with God. The Hebrew mind was not speculative; it moved in the empirico-logical stage of thought, that is, in the realm of the experiential. The world of matter was regarded as alive, full of energy. There was no secondary causation; God was himself the Author of heaven and earth, and of everything observable therein. Moreover, he was the Controller of life in accordance with his covenant stipulations. There was no time when God was not, and no conceivable time when he would cease to be. The Psalmist's declaration expressed quite well the thought of the early chapters of Genesis: "From everlasting to everlasting thou art . . ." (Ps. 90:2).

The question about the existence of God is not raised categorically in the Hebrew Bible. He just was; to argue the point would have been folly. "The churl thinks God does not exist" (Ps. 14:1); his voice and work were evident on all sides. It is then no wonder that when men began to inquire about the origin and meaning of certain great universal facts they traced it all back to God, the Creator.

The Framework of the Tradition

The Bible is composed of many books. Most of those in the Old Testament are composite, having been put together by a masterly hand or hands. No argument is necessary to establish that fact. It is obvious to the observant reader that much of the material is poetic in character and was transmitted orally over a long period of time. The great Mesopotamian saga of creation (the *Enuma elish* = "When on high") is poetic in form and character, and that is doubtless the way Israel's traditions were handed down. So was the Babylonian flood story (Tablet XI of the Gilgamesh Epic). There are still evident a few poetic passages in the Genesis narrative of creation. For example, there is the simple, yet profound, statement that

> God created   the man in his image,
> In the image of God he created him,
> Male and female   he created them.
> . . . .
> Be fruitful and increase   fill up the earth and master it,
> And rule over   the fish of the sea,
> And over the birds of the heavens and over every living creature
> That creeps upon the earth.   (Gen. 1:27–28)

And the ejaculation of the man when he saw the woman Yahweh had made for him:

> This one finally is bone of my bone and flesh of my flesh,
> So this one shall be called woman for she was taken from
>   man.   (Gen. 2:23)

The divine curse upon the serpent, the woman, and the man is mostly poetic in both character and form. God speaks:

To the serpent Because you did this
      You shall be separated
  From all domestic cattle
      And from all wild animals;
  On your belly you will creep
      And eat dust
  All the days of your life.
  And I will put hostility
      Between you and the woman,
  Between your progeny
      And hers.
  They will batter
      Your head
  And you will lunge
      At their heel.

To the woman I will greatly intensify
      Your childbearing pain;
  In pain you will bear children;
      You will have a passionate desire for your
          husband,
        Though he will be your superior.

To the man Perverse will be the land because of you,
      In agony will you eat its produce
        As long as you live.
  Thorns and briars
      It will produce for you
        And you will have to eat cereals.

> By the sweat of your brow
>   You will get bread,
> Until you return to the ground,
>   For you were taken from it;
> For you are dust
>   And to dust you will return.
>
> (Gen. 3:14b-19)

One of the oldest poems in Genesis is the Song of Lamech in Genesis 4:23:

> Listen to me,
>   O wives of Lamech,
> Pay attention
>   To my word,
> Because I slew a man for hurting me
>   And a child for striking me,
> If sevenfold Cain be avenged,
>   Surely Lamech seventy-seven.

Such poetic reminiscences embedded in the present narratives point clearly to an oral tradition by which they were transmitted, in the same way as those of surrounding peoples. But these great universal traditions are now manifestly in prose which reflects writing as the means by which they were finally preserved for posterity. Moreover, these stories were doubtless used in worship, or at least told at the religious centers of the nation. What we have now represents the culmination of an extended process of composition continuing over hundreds of years. In that way basic traditions were preserved, refined and handed down, as may be seen from the deposit of several stories of single events, juxtaposed (the creation narratives) or conflated (the flood stories).

Difficulties of interpretation frequently arise because Western categories of thought are generally employed to explain the meaning of orientally conceived material. Or, to put it another way, formal logical principles are used to elucidate what is essentially poetic portrayal. These early traditions are presented to us within a narrative framework, in terms of picture and story rather than in terms of ideas. The compiler of Genesis 1–11 really paints a vivid, colorful and living portrait of truth embodied in the story of Creation, the Garden in Eden, the Fall, and judgment upon sin. The Bible is neither a book of science nor of philosophy; it is a book of religion and must be interpreted as such—and always with an awareness of its orientalisms in story form.

The Content of the Tradition

The chapters with which we are concerned have to do with origins. The creation stories center about the activity of God in the inception of the heavens and the earth, light, vegetation, planets, insects, birds, marine creatures, land animals and man. Everything in heaven and on earth was called into being by the word of God. "Without him was not anything made that was made" (John 1:3).

It must have been observed by Bible readers that we often have two versions of the same story or event, a fact that can be explained by the one being used at one shrine, the other at another. Scholars have discerned several documents underlying our present Pentateuch, one of them (J = Yahwistic) originating in the early period of the United Kingdom (time of David or Solomon), another (E = Elohistic) in the Northern Kingdom around the shrines at Bethel and Dan established by Jeroboam I

(922–901 B.C.) to provide national worship centers for his people after the disruption of the old Solomonic kingdom.

The later documents had the same general purposes—to provide direction in worship and life in specific historical situations. The work of the Deuteronomist (known as D)—Deuteronomy to II Kings—represents the application of the Mosaic laws and the lessons of history to national problems in the last quarter of the seventh and the first quarter of the sixth centuries in a valiant attempt to save the nation from catastrophe.

The aim of the priestly writer (known as P), to whom we owe the finished product of the first four books of the Bible, was to interweave history and law for purposes of instruction and guidance of the Jewish community in the exilic and postexilic periods. The writer used earlier documents (J and E), incorporating and combining at times and simply copying at others. Some materials he rewrote. Sometimes he used still other sources at his disposal. However, the accent of creation falls upon man who occupies the paramount position in both stories.

P's story of creation (Gen. 1:1–2:4a)	J's story of creation (Gen. 2:4b–25)
1 Earth is formless	1 Earth a waterless waste, devoid of vegetation
2 Creation of light	
3 Division of light and darkness	2 Mist waters the earth
	3 Creation of man
4 Creation of firmament	4 Garden in Eden created for man
5 Appearance of dry land	
6 Creation of grass, herbs and fruit trees	5 Designation of trees and the tree of life

7 Creation of planets
8 Creation of insects, birds, and marine creatures
9 Creation of animals, cattle, etc.
10 Creation of man and woman together

6 Beasts of the field created
7 Woman created as man's companion

From this tabular outline it is clear that two stories are involved. In the first one man stands as the crown of creation; in the second everything produced by the Creator's hand is for his use. In the older story man is recognized as a kind of composite creature—dust from the ground molded by the hand of God and inbreathed by him. The later one makes no mention of dust or of anything suggesting manual activity on the part of the Creator. But there is "the image and likeness of God," which expression, incidentally, ought not be pressed too hard to force upon it a meaning not intended by the author.

God exercises special care for this man by placing him in "a garden in Eden," that is, in a protected place in the steppe, where he is charged with the obligation "to work it and to take care of it" (2:15). Special attention was directed by the Lord to two trees in the midst of the garden. While the full significance escapes us, it does appear that their identification aroused the curiosity of Eve and Adam, and afforded them the opportunity of exercising their freedom of choice, though perhaps not altogether aware of the consequences involved. Disobedience is like that. The result was expulsion from the garden which means that man now became fully human; he was, in a way, on his own. His choice of the tree of the knowledge of good and evil means

that man chose what we might now describe as the human way
with its potentialities and responsibilities. Human life would
henceforth beget human life. Obstacles would have to be overcome. Divisions and disagreements arose within the family along
occupational and even religious lines. Pressed too far they led to
murder—as obsessions and jealousies often do.

This is illustrated by the Cain and Abel story (Gen. 4) with
its many ramifications and which revolves around the theories of
animal and vegetable sacrifice. Cain was a farmer who, in the
course of the fulfillment of his religious obligations, brought a
cereal offering to Yahweh. Abel was a shepherd who also
brought an offering to Yahweh consisting of the best of his flock.
It has been suggested that Cain's offering was rejected because
(1) of his attitude (cf. Ps. 4:5), (2) there was some blemish
involved, (3) of the preference for animal sacrifice, or (4) of
the occupation of the shepherd. In ancient Sumeria the shepherd
was rejected while the farmer was loved and accepted—possibly
because agriculture was the favored occupation in Lower Mesopotamia. However, the chief purpose of the story is probably
theological, showing us the origin, weight and consequences of
sin. Clearly evident are the nature of temptation and how it is
to be resisted ("if you do good"—Gen. 4:7a), the end of uncon-
trolled temper, steps in crime, need for sincerity in offerings,
God's concern even for the guilty sinner, the interdependence
of the members of the human family, and duties and obligations
men owe to one another. The author of the story was vitally
concerned about the tragedies of human life attendant upon
separation from God and the desire to "go it alone." It is no accident that more is said about Cain than about the "righteous
sacrifice" of Abel. Cain was the victim of sin and the Bible has

much to say about God's interest in the sinner and his ceaseless efforts to get him to mend his ways. Jesus affirmed that "there will be more joy in heaven over one sinner who repents than over ninety-nine righteous persons who need no repentance" (Luke 15:7). That is why even in his land of wandering Cain bore the mark of God as an emblem of protection.

The birth of Seth, who ostensibly took the place of Abel, marked a new beginning. But sin was an established fact since Adam's and Eve's disobedience in the garden in Eden and Cain's murder of Abel, as may be seen from the Flood story which is more than a Hebrew version of a universal flood tradition. Virtually nothing is known of the times between Seth and Noah. We have two genealogical traditions in Genesis 4:17–5:22 which purport to trace the intervening families. Interestingly enough, the older of these traditions is Cainite, that is, it follows the line of Cain. The other traces descent through Seth. That there is some relation between the two lines is evident from the table on the following page. (Solid lines indicate the same name; broken lines probably a variation of the same.) The Cainite genealogy ends with occupational names, that of Seth with those of the ancestors of the three great divisions of the human race.

The Flood story is introduced by a short reference to the relationship between the "sons of God" and the "daughters of men" which was, in all probability, meant to explain the progress of mankind as attested by the megalithic monuments that—so they thought—could only have been constructed by superhuman efforts ("those were the days when the Nephilim [= giants] inhabited the earth"—Gen. 6:4). But that this situation was doubtless regarded as a prelude to the Flood story seems apparent

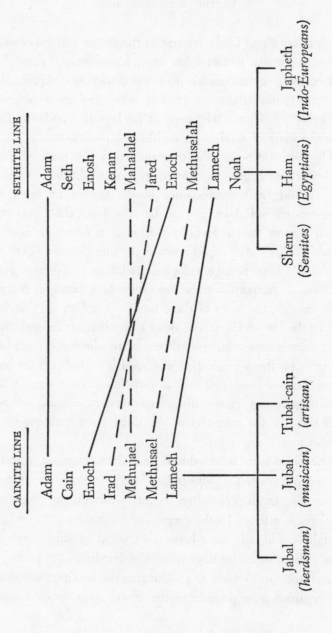

CAINITE LINE

Adam
Cain
Enoch
Irad
Mehujael
Methusael
Lamech

Jabal
(herdsman)   Jubal
(musician)   Tubal-cain
(artisan)

SETHITE LINE

Adam
Seth
Enosh
Kenan
Mahalalel
Jared
Enoch
Methuselah
Lamech
Noah

Shem
(Semites)   Ham
(Egyptians)   Japheth
(Indo-Europeans)

from the remark, "My spirit will not always protect man" (6:3).

In any event, it represents the Hebrew interpretation of a well-nigh universal phenomenon. The nearest parallel is the Babylonian version, the fullest account of which is to be found in Tablet XI of the famous Gilgamesh Epic. In both stories the Flood was the result of divine displeasure with the activity of human beings. Both revolve around a hero (Noah in the Bible; Utnapishtim in the Babylonian story) who was commanded to build a floating vessel (*tebah* = ark; *elippu* = ship). Animals were taken into the vessels for preservation, though with some variation in number and kind. In both stories the Flood covered the earth. After the recession of the waters, the Babylonian ship landed on Mount Nisir, the Hebrew ark on the mountains of Ararat. Birds were released in both versions to test the extent of the abatement of the waters. After leaving the vessels, both heroes offered sacrifices and were the recipients of divine blessings in the course of whose bestowal the deities involved promised never again to destroy the world by a flood.

That the biblical story is conflated from two Hebrew traditions is clear from incidental variations in the present recension. For example, one story has seven pairs of clean animals (7:1-3) enter the ark; the other has one pair of all creatures (6:19-20). One speaks of the Flood continuing for forty days (7:17), the other of the rise of the waters for one hundred fifty days (7:24).

The Hebrew Flood story is an interpretation of the cosmic reaction against "the wickedness of man" and the perversity of his thoughts or plans (Gen. 6:5). Creation, as envisaged by the writer, can operate only on the principles inherent in it; violation of those principles spells doom. That is the basic lesson of the story. The escape of Noah was due to his uprightness and blamelessness. The destruction of the world population demanded a new beginning. As Yahweh laid upon Adam the responsibility to

> Be fruitful and increase,
> Fill up the earth,
> And master it.
>
> (Gen. 1:28)

so he covenanted with Noah and his sons to replenish the earth.

God blessed Noah and his sons, instructing them to "Be fruitful and increase and fill the earth. Dreadful fear of you will be upon all earthly animals, upon all the birds of the heavens, upon the creeping things of the ground and upon all the fish of the sea—which have been given into your hand. Every living creature shall be yours for food; I have given them all to you, as (earlier) the vegetation. Only you must not eat flesh still having its lifeblood in it. . . . You must be fruitful and increase, be productive in the earth and multiply in it." God said further to Noah and his sons together, "See, I am now going to establish my covenant with you and your progeny after you, and with every living animal with you, with bird, with beast, and with every earthly animal with you, every one that came out of the ark—with every earthly animal. And I am going to establish my covenant with you to the effect that never again will all flesh be destroyed by the waters of a deluge, nor shall there again be a flood to devastate the earth. . . .

> This is the sign of the covenant
> Which I am about to make
> Between me and you,
> And between every living being
> Which is with you,
> For all time to come.
> My bow will I put in the clouds,
> And it shall be a covenantal sign
> Between me and the earth."
>
> (Gen. 9:1–13)

The Tower story retains and carries forward the concept of the universal control of God and takes a step further the origin narrative. Hidden within its complexities are signs that man had learned a lesson from the preceding experiences. As André Parrot (*The Tower of Babel* [New York, 1955], pp. 68 f.) has suggested, the tower was not an act of defiance against God. It was originally what the name Babel signified—the gate of God (*bab-ili*). The Hebrews, hearing the word *bab-ili*, connected the phrase with their own word *bālal* (= to confuse), and interpreted the episode as marking the origin of different languages—the confusion of tongues—so that the builders were compelled to cease work because they could no longer communicate with one another. Then their defiant enterprise fell into ruins. The great ziggurats,* of which the tower is a reminiscence, were the bond of union between earth and sky and were meant to assure communication between heaven and earth. They were the first cathedrals. Two stories are thus involved—one describing the tower as the gate of God, the other the confusion of tongues. To maintain communication with God is essential but man cannot reach him by or through material structures. It can take place only when the outstretched hand of man is grasped by the sustaining hand of God.

* The ziggurats were the gigantic stepped structures on the plains of Mesopotamia with which the Hebrew ancestors were undoubtedly familiar and the ruins of some of which may still have been in existence during the period of the Exile. Certainly the exiles must have gazed with amazement on the ruins of others whose condition they may have attributed to the direct intervention of God.

III

ABRAHAM OUR FATHER
(Genesis 12–50)

The phrase "Abraham our father" occurs a dozen times in the
New Testament where it is used by Jesus (Matt. 3:9; Luke
3:8), Zechariah (Luke 1:55), Stephen (Acts 7:2), Paul (Rom.
4:1) and the Jews (John 8:53). It is, of course, an expression
of ancestral relationship, a very important matter in the Semitic
world and one which plays a significant role in both Testaments.
A glance at the genealogies in I Chronicles and Ezra-Nehemiah,
the census lists in Numbers 26, the allotment documents in
Joshua 13–21, and the genealogy of the ancestors of Jesus recorded in Matthew 1:1–16 and Luke 3:23–38 illustrates the
point. A cursory examination of a concordance will demonstrate
the prominence of Abraham for Jews and Christians. Muslims
refer to him as "the friend of God" (Qur'an, Surah 4). Hebron
is called *al-Khalil* (= the friend) and the mosque there is
known by the Arabs as *al-Haram al-Ibrahimi* (= the sanctuary
of Abraham) because it marks the traditional burial place of
Abraham and Sarah.

The Home of Abraham

The early traditions of Genesis (1–11) end with the so-called
confusion of Babel. Two streams of thought now seem to emerge.

The one has to do with the scattering of the human race, with various groups determined to go their own way, following their own inclinations. The other centers in the line of Abraham our father from whose loins comes the tradition of faith in Yahweh and who is regarded as the transmitter of his covenant which, for Christians, culminates in Jesus Christ the Saviour of mankind.

The story of the section of Genesis (12–50) with which we are concerned in this chapter begins in Mesopotamia and ends in Egypt. Between those two geographical foci the drama of Hebrew life and history is played—sometimes the actors get almost entirely off the stage, spilling over at times into Egypt, at others into Mesopotamia. The leading actor in the first scene is Abraham whose traditional home was Mesopotamia. The Bible connects him closely with Aram-naharaim (Aram of the Two Rivers), the geographical region of Upper Mesopotamia whose precise limits varied from period to period. It was always more or less a corridor between east and west and was frequented by all sorts of groups on the move—rarely fixed. Abraham was a product of that vast cultural milieu known as the Fertile Crescent.

Doubtless by virtue of that fact, the ancestral traditions of the Bible bear such a marked resemblance to the creation, flood and other similar stories preserved in the cuneiform documents dug up out of the various mounds in the Tigris-Euphrates Valley, notably the one at Nineveh where the great library of King Ashurbanipal (669–627/6 B.C.) was located. Tablets containing portions of the story of creation were dug up at Nineveh, Ashur and Kish. Most of the cuneiform version of the Flood story in the Gilgamesh Epic comes from Nineveh, though fragments have been found elsewhere, notably at Boghazköy, the Hittite capital in Asia Minor, and at Megiddo. The Adapa myth deal-

ing with man's unsuccessful attempt to gain immortality comes
from El Amarna in Egypt and from Nineveh. The materials
from the Ashurbanipal library at Nineveh date from the seventh
century B.C., but the sources from which those materials were
copied go back into the second and third millennia B.C., perhaps
earlier. The Hebrew fathers, in all probability, brought along
those stories, refined them in the crucible of their unique experience with the Lord, and made them their own.

Who Abraham Was

Apart from being a Mesopotamian, Abraham was the progenitor
of the Hebrew people, as well as of the Arabs. He was the father of Isaac and the grandfather of Jacob. But he was also the
father of Ishmael (16:15; 25:13–16) and the husband (after the
death of Sarah) of Keturah from whom issued, among others, the
South Arabian tribes of Sheba and Dedan (25:1–4).

While the ancestral family connections and exploits of Abraham appear immensely important to the biblical writers, of
much more significance for us is his characterization as a powerful merchant prince and as the father of the faithful.

The Bible associates Abraham with Ur of the Chaldees (in
Lower Mesopotamia) and Haran (in Upper Mesopotamia, on
the Balikh River some seventy miles east of Carchemish). Both
of these places were trade centers at the beginning of the second
millennium B.C. The movements of the patriarch in Mesopotamia, Syria and Canaan, and the enormous wealth attributed
to him in Genesis 13 suggest that he was an extremely successful
merchant. He is said to have been "very rich in livestock, in silver, and in gold" (vs. 2). In fact he and his nephew, Lot, had
so many cattle and sheep that they could not possibly hope to

find enough pasture for them in the same region, "their property was too great for them to live together" (vs. 6).

Archaeological discoveries help us to fill in the details of the biblical narrative and to explain many of the otherwise obscure references and strange customs that were commonplace in Abraham's world and time. For instance, the whole series of practices relating to the birth of Ishmael and the subsequent treatment of Hagar, his mother; the sale of Esau's birthright; Jacob's dealings with his uncle Laban; the household deities; the custom of the deathbed blessing—all are now known to have been normal everyday occurrences regulated by law.

A Nuzi marriage contract provides that a childless wife may take a woman of the country and marry her to her husband to obtain progeny. But she may not drive out the offspring even if she later has children of her own. The child born of the handmaid has the same status as the one born to the wife. That is why, when Sarah wanted to drive out Hagar and Ishmael, it was quite objectionable to Abraham—because of the legal custom of the region from which he came, he was reluctant to do so. It required a special divine dispensation to act contrary to that custom. "And God said to Abraham, 'Do not be disturbed over the lad and your handmaid. Listen to Sarah and do everything she tells you, for in Isaac shall your line (of descent) be perpetuated. As far as the son of the handmaid is concerned, I will make him a great nation too, because he also is your descendant'" (Gen. 21:12–13).

From another Nuzi tablet comes information of the practice of the bartering of a future inheritance to a brother for the price of three sheep. The fact that inheritance rights were transferable from brother to brother helps us to understand Esau's sale of his birthright to Jacob for a mess of stew (Gen. 25:29–34).

Jacob's dealings with Laban, especially in the matter of the household deities, can now be understood in the light of a Kirkuk marriage contract tablet which indicates that the household idols belonged to the son and not to the son-in-law. According to Hurrian law, operative in northern Mesopotamia in the period of the patriarchs, household idols could be the mark of estate rights. Thus Rachel, by possession of the household idols, could insure inheritance rights for her family.

The significance of the blessing which set Jacob and Esau at variance may be judged from a Nuzi legal record according to which two brothers contested the right of a younger brother to a very attractive slave girl. It was brought out in court that the father on his deathbed had blessed his youngest son and thus conferred upon him the right to the slave girl. The gods were invoked to attest the truth of the matter after which the older brothers withdrew their proceedings, thus recognizing the validity of the father's act. The blessing was, therefore, a kind of last will and testament. Isaac had bequeathed to Jacob his blessing in a sort of covenantal ceremony, and even though it was obtained by palpable fraud it could not be changed.

Abraham was thus far from being a half-civilized nomad subject to the whims and fancies of those among whom he moved. He was a wise, shrewd, powerful caravan trader carrying on his business at every important trading post in the land. He is reported to have frequented Damascus, Shechem, Bethel, Hebron and Gerar, all of which were important trade emporia in his time. Genesis 20:1 informs us that he was a resident alien at Gerar where his family was domiciled while he plied his trade of caravaning "between Kadesh and Shur" (= wall [of Egypt]) in the Sinai region.

Father of the Faithful

The patriarchal stories are enmeshed in traditions, customs and practices current in the period in which the Bible places them (twenty-first–nineteenth centuries B.C.). The whole situation surrounding Abraham is of incalculable significance; it is the geographical, ethnological and cultural matrix in which the faith and faithfulness of the father of the faithful was generated and nurtured. Paul has much to say about the faith of Abraham (Rom. 4; Gal. 3), and he was doubtless right in stressing the faithfulness and devotion of the hero of faith, for those are exactly his qualities as reflected in the Genesis story. The expression "God of your fathers" occurs quite often in the Pentateuch and was far more than a pious recognition of the ancestral faith. The "God of the fathers" was the family deity who protected Abraham wherever he went. Genesis 14 narrates clearly the power and position of Abraham, achieved under the protection of his God. Abraham's faithfulness to his God has become an article of faith; the fact that by the help of his God he was able to repulse and defeat the kings of the east already reflects a practical monotheism so apparent in the religion of Moses. The story of Abraham and his immediate successors—especially Jacob and Joseph—depicts a far broader and universal religious outlook than a surface reading of it would indicate.

The Genesis narrative of Abraham reflects both an expansion and limitation in the conception of God. Yahweh became Abraham's God who summoned him to leave his ancestral home for a new land to be shown him and which would, in due time, become the homeland of his descendants. The summons probably came to Abraham in the broad context of human activity, for he was a great merchant prince. But at the same time God elected

Abraham, he demonstrated himself to be a God who was powerful to carry out his will anywhere in the world. Everywhere Abraham went his God went with him. He acted for him wherever and whenever the situation demanded it and hence demonstrated himself to be more than a local deity. Abraham heard him in Ur of the Chaldees, at Harran, at Damascus, at Gerar, and elsewhere. He was by his side in Egypt too. So too the God of the fathers went with Jacob to Aram-naharaim and with Joseph to Egypt just as he had accompanied Abraham from Ur to the far reaches of Canaan and Egypt.

IV

OUT OF EGYPT I CALLED MY SON
(Exodus 1–19)

No biblical tradition is more firmly fixed than the one centering about Israel's sojourn in Egypt. According to the Bible, both Abraham and Isaac had contact with Egypt, mainly in the border districts between the land of Canaan and the country of the Nile. But the migration of Israel to Egypt came in the time of Jacob and was brought on by a famine in Canaan. The story of Joseph tells of the providential care of Yahweh for his people. What appeared at first blush as a terrible tragedy in Jacob's family— the selling of Joseph to a company of itinerant Ishmaelite traders who in turn disposed of him to a wealthy Egyptian family in the service of the Pharaoh—was God's way of preparing for the salvation of his people in a time of devastating famine in southern Palestine. Joseph eventually became vizier of Egypt and as such brought his people to the land of Goshen—in the eastern apex of the Nile Delta—where they settled and carried on their occupation as shepherds and herdsmen.

At the invitation of the Pharaoh, Jacob and his sons are reported to have taken up residence in Egypt.

Pharaoh said to Joseph, "Tell your brothers: Do this: Load up your beasts of burden and hurry to the land of Canaan. Then gather up your father and your families and come to me. I'll

give you the most fertile district in the land of Egypt where you can eat the fat of the land. Furthermore, you must instruct them: Do this: Take wagons from the land of Egypt for the transportation of your children, your wives, and your father, and return. Don't concern yourselves about your goods, for you shall have the most fertile district in the whole land of Egypt."
(Gen. 45:17–20)

The Pharaoh's directive to Joseph was more explicit when Jacob and his sons arrived in the land.

Your father and your brothers have come to you; the land of Egypt is yours. Domicile your father and your brothers in the very best of the land; let them take up residence in the land of Goshen.   (Gen. 47:5b–6a)

The book of Exodus begins with Israel in Egypt and her deliverance from bondage, and ends with the majestic scene at Mount Sinai.

Israel in Egypt

The political fortunes of any nation are bound to change, even those of a relatively stable and protected one like Egypt. Israel in Egypt was the victim of dynastic change. She was caught in that nation's violent reaction against foreigners who had invaded the Nile Valley earlier. Instead of living a quiet and peaceful life in the rich pasture land of Goshen, the people of Israel suddenly found themselves enslaved—an obnoxious condition for a pastoral people. Their camps were placed under strict surveillance and, had it not been for sympathetic treatment by Egyptian midwives, they might have been wiped out by infanticide. Yet somehow the corvée has a way of producing virility and fertility —"the people multiplied and increased very greatly" (1:20).

The Egyptian authorities might well fear a strong and numerous foreign population located just in the territory through which alone invading armies from the east could approach and enter their country. Should the Hebrews develop an effective leader, they could easily join forces with hostile powers and so repeat the catastrophe that had overtaken the land in the time of the Hyksos when Egypt was overrun by Asiatics between ca. 1800–1550 B.C. in what amounted to a great national humiliation. The Egyptian answer to this possibility was extermination by oppression and forced labor. The opportunity for rebellion never came. But through the efforts and under the direction of Moses the Hebrews succeeded in freeing themselves from Egyptian hegemony and embarked upon a course of adventure destined to bring them to the land covenanted by God to their fathers.

Moses

Precisely when the condition of the Hebrew slaves seemed most hopeless, there arose one of the greatest religio-political leaders of all time. Unpropitious circumstances are often used by the Lord to achieve his purposes. It was so now. To a Hebrew slave family, Amram and Jochebed (Ex. 6:20), was born a son who, by the strangest coincidence, was delivered from the murderous hands of the royal agents and educated at the very court that had undertaken to destroy every Hebrew male child. The author of the Epistle to the Hebrews (11:23–29) was right in observing that it all happened through "faith," or perhaps we might say through the faithfulness of God who had entered into covenant with the fathers.

Stephen opines that "Moses was instructed in all the wisdom of the Egyptians, and was mighty in words and deeds" (Acts 7:22). Just so, for he clearly exhibits something of that wisdom in his relationship with his own people and in his handling of the Pharaoh and his advisers. Even while connected with the court, he maintained a deep sense of allegiance to his people as may be seen from intervention on behalf of one of them who happened to be belabored by an Egyptian taskmaster. "At that time, when he had grown up, Moses went out to his brothers and observed their forced labor. Seeing an Egyptian striking one of his Hebrew brothers, he looked all around and when he saw no one, he slew the Egyptian and hid his body in the sand" (Ex. 2:11–12). Public knowledge of that act precipitated hasty flight to the desert of Sinai whence he fell in with a priest of Midian who befriended him and eventually gave him his daughter Zipporah as wife. Taking up the desert occupation of shepherding, he tended his father-in-law's sheep in the steep ravines and mountain passes of Sinai.

So he might well have passed the rest of his days in comparative contentment had it not been for an unusual experience. As Rudolph Kittel once wrote, "In the silent loneliness of the endless desert he came to know his God."* However one may explain the phenomena surrounding that experience, he cannot explain away the experience itself. Moses met the Lord and, as in Jacob's wrestle with the angel, the Lord prevailed. What transpired in that awesome moment was simply that the Spirit of God impressed Moses so overwhelmingly that he was constrained to return to the task in Egypt for which he had been only partially prepared earlier and which he had hastily relinquished when his covert acts in behalf of his brethren were noised abroad.

Shepherding in the quiet desert with its awe-inspiring sights

* *Great Men and Movements in Israel* (New York, 1929), p. 30.

afforded time and opportunity for Moses to meditate, to think through the plight of his brothers in Egypt and to re-evaluate the possibility of his intervention. Though he was not smitten to the ground, like Paul on the Damascus way, his reluctance was overcome by divine revelation. The One who spoke to him out of the burning bush was the God of the fathers, the One who had called and protected Abraham, who was the Kinsman of Isaac (Gen. 31:42), and the Companion of Jacob. He was the Creator God, the Protector of the faithful and would now be also the Redeemer of those in slavery and bondage.

Deliverance

Though the task laid upon him was manifestly repugnant to him, Moses relented, put aside his qualms and made his way back to Egypt. The only assurance he had was the sign of the mountain (Ex. 3:12). His mission would be complete only when his people worshiped in the sanctuary where he had received his call. Hence it was that he set out *in faith* on the mission to lead Israel out of servitude, weld them together into a people of God, and bring them to the temple of Sinai to receive the covenant.

The contest between the Lord and the Pharaoh (who was himself regarded as god) initiated by the former through Moses had both immediate and far-reaching repercussions. Evidently not all of the Israelites wanted to be delivered; they enjoyed the fleshpots of Egypt. Moses had to contend with at least a partially reluctant people as well as with a recalcitrant monarch. And the contest was not over when the Pharaoh agreed to let Israel go. For the moment the Lord had prevailed over the god of Egypt, but the worst was still to come. A few days after Israel departed, the Pharaoh had a change of heart. Perhaps he had thought the motley crew of erstwhile slaves would soon be overcome by the desert, repent and return. When that did not happen, he set out with his army to bring them back. The mighty hand of the Lord operative in forcing the King to capitulate now appeared to have lost its punch. Encamped on the shore of the Sea of Reeds, their attention was suddenly attracted by a rising cloud of dust and the clatter of chariot wheels. That was exactly what the less hardy souls, opponents of Moses and Aaron, expected. Now they were caught between an irresistible force and a seemingly immovable object. They could not flee into the desert, for the hosts of the Pharaoh blocked the way. Nor could they advance because in front of them lay the marshes of the sea. As always, however, when human resources run out, God intervened. He made a way of escape for his people and, as he had promised Moses, they never saw the face of the Pharaoh again.

Poets and psalmists of Israel ever afterward sang about that great deliverance. It became the chief article in their creed. The salvation poem of Moses became the theme song of the nation.

> I will sing to Yahweh,
> For he has been utterly triumphant.
> Horse and driver he has tossed into the sea.
> Yahweh is my strength and my song,
> He has proved (to be) my salvation.
>
> (Ex. 15:1-2)

V

I AM THE LORD THY GOD
(Exodus 20)

In the preceding chapter reference was made to the fact that Moses was commissioned to bring Israel out of Egypt and that, although his task was not quite finished when the people encamped at Mount Sinai, the sign of the completion of the main portion of his mission was marked by their worship of God "at this mountain" (Ex. 3:12). Actually, at that moment, deliverance had already taken place. The promise of the Lord to Moses had been fulfilled. It remained but to spell out for Israel its meaning more precisely.

Order of Events

The order of events narrated in the first half of the book of Exodus is often ignored by commentators. A bare outline of the more important ones may be helpful at this point.

1 Oppression of Israel in Egypt.
2 Birth and first period of the education of the deliverer.
3 Intervention in the affairs of his people forces his flight to Midian.
4 Second period of the education of Moses, including his call.
5 Return to Egypt to carry out his commission.
6 The execution of the commission with its repercussions.

7 Death of Egyptian first-born, Hebrew Passover, and depar-
   ture from Egypt.
8 The appearance of the pillar of fire and cloud.
9 Deliverance from the Pharaoh and the Reed Sea.
10 Further journey from Reed Sea to Mount Sinai.
11 Arrival at Mount Sinai.
12 Revelations at Mount Sinai.

Freedom from slavery, from the vengeance of the Pharaoh, and
from the threatening perils of the Reed Sea constituted momentous acts of the Lord in the process of the fulfillment of the covenant made to the fathers. They were acts of grace and salvation,
without obligation on his part, except to himself, as embodied
in his promises to Abraham.

Liberation itself came before the covenant stipulations of Sinai were revealed. The helping hand of God was extended to
Israel and Israel grasped that hand unconditionally. Only at Sinai was disclosed what was involved in being the people of the
Lord. That is also the order stressed by Paul in his matchless
Epistle to the Romans. At the old sanctuary of the Lord, the
people of Israel were confirmed into the Lord's covenant with
the fathers.

Revelation of Covenant Stipulations

Response to the first act of grace involved a commitment on
Israel's part, commitment whose terms Jeremiah recalled so vividly some seven hundred years later: "I will be your God and
you shall be my people" (7:23; 11:4; 24:7; 30:22; 32:38). The
constituent elements of the divine economy thus far were election, promise, and deliverance. God had shown himself faithful,
respondent to all he had promised to the fathers. The sons of

the fathers accepted God's offer of grace and deliverance and so regarded themselves as his people par excellence. To be his people, however, meant far more than being called by his name. It entailed a reflection on their part of the same qualities of steadfast love, devotion, loyalty, reliability, faithfulness inherent in their God who had chosen and delivered them. In a word, they must be a holy people because God is holy. "I am Yahweh your God; sanctify yourselves and be holy, for I am holy. . . . For I am Yahweh who brought you up out of the land of Egypt to be your God. Therefore you are to be holy because I am holy" (Lev. 11:44–45; cf. also Lev. 19:2; 20:26).

What did that mean? How was Israel to be different from other people? What were to be the distinguishing marks of Yahweh's people? Here the Bible is clear and precise. Yahweh's people were a saved, redeemed people, whose distinctive characteristics were voiced in "these words." The introduction to both versions of the so-called Decalogue refers to "these words" (Ex. 20:1) or "the word(s) of the Lord" (Deut. 5:5); it does not call them commandments! Both versions begin with a preamble: "I am the Lord your God who brought you out of the land of Egypt, out of the house of slaves." God had delivered Israel and Israel had accepted deliverance. Henceforth Israel was his people.

Between Egypt and the Reed Sea and the Promised Land another stupendous act of God's grace took place. He revealed to his people the kind of world they were about to enter and how they were to react toward it in worship and life. It was a world full of all sorts of temptations, attractions and allurements against which they would have to be on constant guard. In effect this is what God said his people must avoid in Canaan—"Now I am your God. I have acted in your behalf and by your response you have manifested your willingness to be my people. I am about to fulfill my promise to Abraham, to give you the land of Canaan which you must win for yourselves. Nevertheless, I will be with you, to help you, if you continue to accept my guidance and direction.

"In the land you are about to enter you must ever remember that you are my people. The inhabitants have other gods, attractive in appearance and fanatically worshiped. Recall the impotence of the gods of Egypt; the gods of Canaan are equally impotent. Do not be enticed by them. For you they do not exist. Those charming, enchanting idols with their fascinating ceremonials are deceptive. You must not be allured by them.

"Moreover, as my people you know by experience what I am and must not attribute to me what I did not command or what I disapprove. You must not associate with my name anything not consonant with my character or that is against my will. You must not falsely ascribe to me what I did not say or do, or use my name in attesting what is patently untrue.

"You must remember and respect the Sabbath by keeping it holy. You must respect father and mother and accord them due honor and obedience. You must not endeavor in any way to circumvent your responsibility toward them. To do so would fracture the very basis of your family life and undermine your character as my people.

"You must hold the life of all your fellows as sacred. You are covenant brothers, sons of mine. Human life among the people whither you are going is held in contempt and blood is shed with impunity. It must not be so among you. Remember Cain and Abel.

"Marriage is sacred. It is the foundation of your families, the source for the perpetuation of your name. The people of Canaan regard adultery as harmless. It is condoned as a part of their religion. Do not be tempted to follow them even when you are told fertility rites are essential for agricultural pursuits in the land. Inasmuch as I am giving you the land, to be parceled out to each of your tribes and families, you must not treat lightly the property of your brothers. Neither must you pilfer the household chattels nor the blessings accruing to your brothers by virtue of their honest use of my gifts. You must work for yourselves.

"When disputes arise among you and you bring your case before the elders at the gate, be sure your testimony is accurate and true. You are brothers and under no circumstances must you show partiality, violate the canons of truth, or be subject to bribery. Finally, set your heart upon the cultivation of your own allotment, the enjoyment of your family, and the appreciation of your own possessions. Respect your neighbor's blessings, help him to maintain and cultivate them, for in so doing you will enhance your own and fulfill the covenant of brotherhood."

"These words" do not point specifically to a cultic institution. They are covenantal stipulations indicating how Israel is to maintain her relationship with the Lord and how she is to conduct her internal affairs within the covenant community, if she is to be a truly holy people, the Lord's people.

SACRIFICES AND OFFERINGS
(Leviticus 1–16)

Sacrifices and offerings are described in Leviticus, the one book of the Old Testament usually skipped over as rapidly as possible because of its rather dull recital of Hebrew ceremonials that no longer appear to concern Jews or Christians. But perhaps those who so cavalierly step over this book may be passing up a real opportunity to examine the whole rationale of Israel's worship life, how she responded cultically to the Lord's blessings. It may be well to call attention to the order of the Leviticus narrative as it now stands. At the beginning of the book (1–10) stands the summary statement of the cultic observances of the covenant people, the holy people—the statement of their worship response to God. This is followed by a series of health regulations governing the holy community (11–15), and the ritual for the great Day of Atonement (16). Finally there is the "Holiness Code" (17–26) which sets forth principles of conduct for the holy people—they serve as guides for and are descriptive of the qualities of those who have been reconciled to God. These are not laws in the accepted sense of the term; they are rather revelations of the way matters stand for a genuinely covenanted people.

What Sacrifice Is

Sacrifice, in the biblical sense of the term, is an external expression of man's response to the grace of God. In a way it is visible prayer offered to God in terms of his manifold gifts which alone make it possible. The act of sacrifice symbolizes intercommunication between the divine being and his client. A two-way relationship is always presupposed in a successful or complete sacrifice. The offerer presents his oblation, God accepts it and the erstwhile strained or broken relationship is re-established. Otherwise sacrifice would be a meaningless travesty as may be seen from the experience of Cain.

> In the course of time, Cain brought an offering of the produce of the land. . . . But Yahweh disregarded Cain and his offering, so that Cain became very angry and distraught. Then Yahweh said to Cain, "Why are you angry and why are you distraught? Is it not so, that if you act properly you will be favored; but if you do not act properly, sin, whose attraction is for you, is a demon at the door? But you can prevail over him."
>
> (Gen. 4:3–7)

The ordinary Hebrew had no other way of expressing his feelings toward his God. That could be done only by some outward act which carried with it a profound inner significance and whose total impact could not be completely or fully portrayed in words.

Elemental Offerings

Leviticus distinguishes three basic types of offerings, each with its own import and purpose. The first of these types is the burnt offering (ch. 1). This offering is referred to nearly three hundred times in the Old Testament. It could be either public or private in character and it always required a live victim—a bull, a sheep or goat, a turtledove or young pigeon. It is often called a whole burnt offering because the whole animal or bird was consumed on the altar. It signified the total giving of the gift to God; not a part of it was withheld. The special character of this offering made it particularly appropriate for occasions when complete dedication was called for. It has been said that the general prayer in the church service occupies the place of the burnt offering in Israel's sacrificial system.

The second of the great offerings was the vegetable offering (ch. 2) whose materials were choice flour mixed with oil and frankincense, or unleavened cakes with oil, or unleavened wafers spread with oil, or a griddle or pan offering composed of choice flour and oil. The offerer could also present parched grain in season as an offering of first fruits. Unleavened meal indicated the absence of corruption and the seasoning with salt symbolized friendship. The vegetable offering was, in essence, a gift from the worshiper to God.

The third, and, in some respects the most interesting and significant of the elemental offerings, was the peace offering (ch. 3). It was an animal offering—either a bull, sheep or goat. This offering has been labeled a communion offering. The new Jewish translation of the Torah renders the Hebrew word as "a sacrifice of well-being." Careful reading discloses two aspects involved in the peace offering: (a) the portion of the animal offered as a gift to the Lord, and (b) the residue consumed by the cult personnel, the worshiper and his family, and the poor. The Hebrew, unlike other ancient peoples, never conceived of a union with the divine by eating the sacrificial victim. He had another way of achieving fellowship with his God, that is, the way of hospitality. Here in the peace offering was a sharing of the sacrificial victim by the Lord, the priests and the offerer. It signified the existence of a right relation, peace between the participants or, if it had been ruptured, the restoration of the proper religio-family relationship.

In addition to the above were such special offerings as the sin offering (4:1–5:13) and the guilt offering (5:14–6:7). Both of these offerings emphasize the seriousness of sin in the religious economy of the nation, its power to disrupt the covenant community, and the necessity to deal with it resolutely.

Meaning of Sacrifice in Israel

Although this has been pointed out at several places above, it may be well to deal more specifically with a few over-all impressions. The underlying principle of all sacrifice was the positive feeling for the maintenance of the covenant which the Lord had offered his people and which they accepted. Without him there would have been no deliverance from Egypt, no people Israel, no covenant, no revelation of stipulations to guide the covenanted people in the midst of conditions and situations wholly at variance with the nation's experience of the gracious and loving Lord. To maintain a providential relationship with him was imperative, as Israel's religious leaders recognized. For them, the only way that could be done was by a system of symbolic acts referred to as sacrifices and offerings. They too were thought of as revelations of the Lord, who knew what was in man, that he was prone to go his own way to later regret. Hence the Lord provided for his people a way to preserve the covenant as it related to himself and the community.

Given the milieu of Canaan, there were bound to be breakdowns, both personal and national. How else could such predicaments be overcome except by recognition of the wrongs committed and a speedy making of amends—not so much the payment of a penalty as the repair of a rupture? It could be done by a complete rededication as provided for in the burnt offering, by the meal offering with its symbol indicating the removal of corruption and the presence of the salt of friendship, or by the peace offering through which individual and community were reconciled to the Lord. God had indeed provided for his people a way of escape. Only when his gifts of reconciliation were regarded as automatic guarantees of preservation and salvation did the prophets attack them because such attitudes represented a gross misuse of the sacrificial grace of God.

Israel's sacrificial system provided only for the removal or forgiveness of sins committed unwittingly (4:2). There is no ritual for the expiation of sins incurred defiantly, that is, those committed with a high hand (Num. 15:30–31). Such sins were apparently ineradicable, as was blasphemy against the Holy Ghost (Mark 3:29).

THE WAY OF THE WILDERNESS
(Numbers)

The book of Numbers is occupied with more than the census of the various tribes of Israel encamped at Sinai (1–4) and on the plains of Moab (26). The Hebrew name of the book—the initial word or the key word in the first line of each of the books of the Torah becomes its title for the Jews—is "In the wilderness" (*bemidbar Sinai*). Our present title, Numbers, comes from the Septuagint and is derived from the Greek for the phrase "the number of names" in 1:2.

The over-all impression left with the reader is that the compiler of the book was vitally concerned with the fortunes of Israel in the wilderness. The wilderness was the place of wandering, of all kinds of activities and experiences operative in welding a heterogeneous people into a more or less religiously unified entity. Tribal and clan differences were not obliterated but together the tribes became more the children of Israel than the children of Ephraim, Manasseh, Judah, etc. They were united into a tribal confederation known as the twelve tribes of the children of Israel which became almost an article of faith for later writers.

Israel in the Wilderness

The first ten chapters of Numbers tell of the final events at Mount Sinai. They deal for the most part with organizational matters such as a census, ceremonial regulations for the camp, Levitical arrangements in the service of the tabernacle, orders for celebrating the Passover and various signals for use in camp movements. Those were important factors in the tradition but cannot be viewed as outweighing what follows.

The Numbers narrative, after chapter 10, is really concerned with the period referred to in the title since it deals with Israel's movements from Sinai to the camp site at Shittim in the plains of Moab opposite Jericho. Although the material in this section of Numbers is from different structural levels (documents) of unequal value in detail, there cannot be the slightest doubt of the historicity of the nucleus of the stories related. It is just the mixture of all sorts of tales that makes the narrative ring true.

The composition of Numbers continues the pattern exhibited in Genesis and Exodus. The documents noted above appear here too. As in other stories—creation, the flood, and parts of the Abraham story—more than one tradition is evident. That may be due to the conflation of experiences undergone by different segments of Israel at different periods. In Numbers 13:21 the spies are reported to have searched out the whole land of Canaan from "the wilderness of Zin as far as Rehob, at the Hamath entrance." But according to verse 22 they went only as far as Hebron. In the older account, Joshua is not mentioned in the spy story (13:20; 14:24); in the later one (P) both he and Caleb are said to have pacified the people (14:6, 30, 38) and hence escaped the sentence of exclusion from the land decreed for the pessimists.

It is possible to present here only a bare outline of happenings on the way of the wilderness. One of the most striking facts is the series of bitter complaints lodged by the people against the Lord and Moses. They grumbled about a one-dish diet: "O that we might have meat to eat! We recall the fish we ate in Egypt gratis, and the cucumbers, and the watermelons, and the leeks, and the onions, and the garlic. But now we are famished; there is nothing at all except the manna to look at" (11:4d–6). They lamented their predicament in the wake of the report of the spies. "If only we had died in the land of Egypt or in this desert! Why has Yahweh brought us to this land, only to fall by the sword? Our wives and our children will be victimized. Would it not be better for us to return to Egypt?" (14:2c–3). Korah and his associates rebelled openly against Moses and Aaron. They said: "Too much for you! For the whole congregation is holy, all of them, and Yahweh is in their midst. Why do you exalt yourselves above the congregation of Yahweh?" (16:3). They bemoaned the lack of water; between Mount Hor and the road skirting Edom they voiced bitter representations against God and Moses. "The people argued with Moses and complained, 'If only we had perished when our brothers perished before Yahweh! Why have you brought the congregation of Yahweh into the desert where we and our cattle will die? Why have you brought us up from Egypt to this horrid place? It is no place for grain, figs, vines, or pomegranates, and there is no water to drink'" (20:3–5). But whenever they took matters into their own hands, after such outcries, they met with worse misfortune (14:20–45; chs. 17, 21). One of the notable lessons of the wilderness is that God's way is right and that he has time to wait for the next generation (14:20–25). He is concerned about the course of history and life of which any particular moment is but a minute segment.

However, despite the wail of woe chanted through vale after vale of the wilderness, God did not forsake his people. He provided other diet for them, brought water from beneath the rocks, and healed those bitten by poisonous adders. He allowed recalcitrant dissidents to remove themselves, provided for successors to Moses and Aaron, cleared the way to the land of promise by overwhelming Arad, Sihon and Og (ch. 21). Again and again there is the lesson that "the wages of sin is death" and that the gift of life is bestowed on those who accept the discipline of the Lord. G. B. Gray has expressed the opinion that the main thought of Numbers is that "Israel is Yahweh's son and as such the object of his perpetual care and discipline" (*Numbers* [International Critical Commentary: New York, 1903], p. xlviii).

A further aspect of the wilderness experience is the humanness of Moses who stands in intimate relationship with the Lord (12:6–8). On the one hand, he distinguishes himself by his submission to the Lord (12:3), by his trust in him (10:29–32), by such affection for Israel that he intercedes with the Lord on their behalf despite their often hostile attitude toward him (11:2, 10–15; 21:7), and by the display of a genuine spirit of understanding on nearly every occasion when his patience must have been sorely tried. On the other hand, he reflects thoroughly human traits. He is subject to despondency (11:10–15), to anger under provocation (20:9–11) and to human passion (12:1).

The Discipline of the Wilderness

It was no whim or fancy that led the prophets to recall the way of the wilderness and long for a return to it. Thus it is that Hosea speaks nostalgically: "I will allure her, and bring her into the wilderness, and speak tenderly to her" (2:14). There is even more play on this idea in Jeremiah 2. It is no accident that the Lord was looked upon as a God of the wilderness or desert where Israel's men of faith came in contact with him or whither they resorted to renew their faith and strength for the struggle against the Baalistic corruption perennially threatening the nation. Moses met the Lord in the desert, Jacob wrestled with the angel at the Jabbok, Elijah repaired to Horeb before the final battle with Jezebel and her devotees of Baal, and the Psalmists sang often of the Lord's coming from the desert.

Just what was in the mind of Hosea and Jeremiah when they referred so longingly to the wilderness period? Some idealism was certainly present in their sentiments, but far more than that is implied. They saw in the wilderness experience of Israel a proximity between the Lord and his people that was absent in the land of the sown. There he was a God close at hand and, though their youthful impetuosity led to all sorts of serious misadventures, Israel was conscious of his guiding presence, his loving care, his support. Hosea caught the significance of it all:

When Israel was an inexperienced youth,
I fell in love with him.
Out of Egypt I called my son . . .
I taught Ephraim to walk,
Taking them up into my arms . . .
With human cords I led them,
With bonds of love.
I was to them like those who lift a babe to their cheeks,
I bent over them and fed them.   (11:1-4)

That was the divine-human relationship prevalent in the way of the wilderness the prophets wanted to recapture. It was a period of hardship and discipline, but also one with a deep sense of nearness, dependence and love. The priestly festival of *Suk-koth* (= booths or tabernacles) was an attempt to ritualize the wilderness experience (cf. Deut. 16:13–15; Lev. 23:33–43; Num. 29:12–38; and the Mishnah Tractate Sukkah). Later it was connected with the feast of the ingathering and included a study of the Torah (Neh. 8:13–9:5). The importance of the wilderness for even the postexilic prophets may be seen from the eschatological vision of Zechariah 14:16–19. To judge from the history of Israel, the religious festival failed to recover effectively for the people that relationship with the Lord which Hosea envisioned.

VIII

A LAND FLOWING
WITH MILK AND HONEY
(Joshua)

The way of the wilderness came to an end as Israel set up camp across the Jordan from Jericho. When Moses climbed Mount Nebo to survey the Promised Land he knew that his period of service was about to terminate. But he had the good fortune of seeing the people of the Lord on the threshold of the land that would henceforth be their own. What he thought of that land we do not know; that is a secret he carried to his grave. To be sure it must have looked somewhat more inviting than much of the territory Israel had seen since leaving Goshen but, if he saw what the present-day traveler sees from the same eminence, he must have been a bit disappointed.

The Land of Canaan

Traditionally Canaan was referred to as "a land flowing with milk and honey" (cf. Josh. 5:6) and compared to the wilderness in which Israel spent nearly forty years it was doubtless attractive. It was truly a land of promise in more than one respect but a great deal of effort and determination would be required to fulfill the expectations in the mind of the writer who coined that glowing description. Taken as a whole, however, the land had some possibilities, though it could not compare with the land of Egypt or the fertile areas of the Mesopotamian valleys.

The Deuteronomist spoke of it as "a land of hills and valleys, which drinks water by the rain from heaven, a land which Yahweh your God cares for" (Deut. 11:11–12) and "a good land, a land of brooks of water, of fountains and springs, flowing forth in valleys and hills, a land of wheat and barley, of vines and fig trees and pomegranates, a land of olive trees and honey, a land in which you will eat bread without scarcity, in which you will lack nothing, a land whose stones are iron and out of whose hills you can dig copper" (8:7–9). It was the land of "the pride of the Jordan" (Zech. 11:3), the luxuriant growth in the valley that betokened fertility and promise, as may be seen even today from the banana groves, the stately palm orchards, and prolific melon fields. There was the Plain of Esdraelon, running eastward from Mount Carmel to the Jordan, with its grain fields, the Plain of Sharon with its vineyards and flowers and the Valley of Eshcol, near Hebron, over which the spies waxed so eloquent. The existence of Canaanite cities by the water courses was ample evidence of the productive capabilities of the land. Moreover, as Nelson Glueck's surface explorations have shown, there were copper and iron ore deposits in the hills bordering the Valley of the Aqabah. The potentialities of the land may be seen from the later exploits of King Solomon under whom prosperity reigned in almost every corner.

Occupancy of the Land

Proof of the resources of the land was demonstrated by the apparent strength and virility of its inhabitants. While the Canaanites were not really giants, they did have walled cities and were equipped to fight. They were strong and well fed, and seemingly well organized. That was especially true of the valley dwellers whom Israel could not dislodge easily. Again and again (Judg. 1:27, 29, 30, 31, 33) it is said that Manasseh, Ephraim, Asher, Zebulun, and Naphtali "could not drive out the inhabitants" of the land. At Shittim the Hebrews became restive and desirous of entering upon their promised land. The desert wanderings brought them closer together, forged an organization and discipline essential for conquest. But it also produced an irrepressible yearning for the blessings in store for them on the other side of the Jordan River.

Before they set out on the final stage of achieving their objective, the Israelites were afforded another manifestation of the power and providence of God. The pillar of cloud and fire had disappeared. The Ark of the Covenant now took on a new function; it became the symbol of the divine presence.

The Ark of the Covenant was, doubtless, a purely Israelite symbol. The Bible traces it to Moses who instructed Bezalel to construct it (Ex. 31:2; 35:30; 36:1; 37:1). According to Exodus 37:1–9, he made it after Moses returned from his conversations with Yahweh on Mount Sinai. Later tradition had it that the Ark contained a pot of manna, Aaron's rod, and the tablets of the commandments (Heb. 9:4). Scholars have pointed out that the Ark signified the divine presence, that it became a sacred palladium symbolizing Yahweh's presence in war (I Sam. 4), that it was the repository of a fetish stone from Sinai or of the commandment tablets, and that it represented the portable throne of the invisible deity. It occupied a rather significant role in the wilderness, in the early tribal amphictyony centered at Shiloh, and in the period of the monarchy under David. Little is heard of it after that because it was placed in the Holy of Holies in the Solomonic temple, out of public view.

Though the Jordan which stood between them and their immediate goal was in flood, when the priests bearing the Ark approached the stream its waters were cut off so that the people crossed over on dry ground. Perhaps the natural damming of the waters above Jericho was the proximate cause of the phenomenon, but its occurrence at that moment was interpreted as an act of God. That is what Joshua meant when he set up the memorial stones at Gilgal (Josh. 4:1–24). It confirmed the people in the belief that the Lord was with Joshua as he had been with Moses.

From Gilgal Israel's new captain surveyed the situation and consolidated his forces. Since the manna had ceased (Josh. 5:12), the people helped themselves to the produce of the land. They could not proceed, however, until they had all rededicated themselves to the purpose of the Lord; only then could they take possession of the land. Without much difficulty Jericho, the key city standing athwart the gateway to the central highland, fell before the hosts of Israel. It was devoted as an offering of first fruits to the Lord, but not all of it. Achan yielded to temptation and claimed a part of it for himself—a breach of faith with the Lord, a problem with which the nation had to contend ever after. The Deuteronomist blamed it for the crushing defeat suffered in the first attempt at invasion of the highlands, which may have been due rather to pride and overconfidence in their own ability.

The battle took place somewhere between Bethel and Ai (= ruin); Israel was put to flight and it was only after the tragic purge of Achan and a realistic assessment of the situation that progress continued. Bethel was destroyed by a tremendous conflagration in the first half of the thirteenth century B.C. and other cities such as Makkedah, Libnah, Lachish, Eglon, Debir—

all cities in the low hill country to the southwest of Jerusalem—
soon followed (10:28–42). The Gibeonite tetrapolis (a league
of the four Canaanite cities of Gibeon, Chephirah, Beeroth and
Kirjath-jearim located within a radius of eight to ten miles north
and northwest of Jerusalem) was held in check by treaty, to the
chagrin of the Israelite chiefs when they discovered the ruse by
which it was obtained (ch. 9). There is some evidence for a
northern campaign (ch. 11), but the fertile plains of Sharon,
Accho and Esdraelon remained in Canaanite hands. It is fairly
certain that the central highland from the southern boundary of
Esdraelon to the Negeb was in Israelite control by the end of the
thirteenth century.

Final Days of Joshua

Joshua had performed his task well. Israel had more than a foothold in the land and it had developed a sense of common operation that enabled its hosts to carry out further plans of conquest,
however slowly and painfully. The portion of the land awaiting
occupancy is described in Joshua 13:1–6. In spite of the enormous task ahead, the nation could well give thanks to the Lord
for what Joshua had accomplished. In customary fashion the
valiant leader is reported to have concluded his period of service
with a lengthy address at Shechem (ch. 24) in which he exhorted
the people to fear the Lord and continue in his way.

Speaking to the assembled tribes of Israel and their leaders,
Joshua rehearsed the story of Yahweh's direction of his people
since the time of Abraham and then admonished them:

Now, then, reverence Yahweh and serve him in complete
loyalty. Renounce the gods your fathers worshiped across the
river and in Egypt; worship Yahweh. If it appears wrong to
you to worship Yahweh, then decide for yourselves this very day

whom you want to worship—whether the gods your fathers worshiped across the river, or the gods of the Amorites in whose land you live. As for me and my family, we will worship Yahweh.

The response of the assembly was equally vigorous:

Far be it from us to abandon Yahweh in order to worship other gods, for it was Yahweh our God who brought us and our fathers up out of the land of Egypt, out of slavery, performing before our very eyes these great signs and keeping us every step of the way we went among all the nations whose territory we crossed. Moreover, Yahweh drove out all the nations—together with the Amorites—who inhabited the land before us. Yes, we too will worship Yahweh, for he is our God.

(24:14–18)

Though the farewell discourses are typically Deuteronomic in character, there can hardly be a doubt that a covenant ceremony did take place at Shechem in which the participants bound themselves to remain faithful to the Lord and to proceed in the furtherance of their objective in the spirit of Joshua. The "land flowing with milk and honey" was firmly within the grasp of Israel when he departed.

IX

STRUGGLE FOR A HOMELAND
(Judges)

By the time Joshua relinquished his position at Shechem, Israel had gained a firm foothold in the land. But the campaign was by no means over. Even the central highland was still vulnerable, especially along the main highways. Actually the conquest was not completed until the time of David (1000–962 B.C.), and hence was a long drawn-out process extending over a period of two and a half centuries. Allotment did not automatically carry with it factual possession; that required arduous effort on the part of the families and clans making up the several tribes. That is what was meant by the Lord's declaration to Joshua: "You are old and advanced in years, and there appears yet very much land to be possessed" (Josh. 13:1).

The Book of Judges

The book of Judges, as it now stands, carries forward the story of Israel's occupancy of Canaan. It has been said that settlement began with Abraham, and Isaac and Jacob appeared pretty much at home there. The book of Jubilees (ch. 34) reflects conquest in the time of Jacob. The problem is an enormously complex one and those scholars who hold that not all Israel was in Egypt may have a point. At any rate, Judges shows activity on a wide

front and ought perhaps to be characterized as the story of consolidation and expansion of positions occupied from patriarchal
times on or won under Joshua.

Our present book combines a whole series of events transmitted to us within a so-called Deuteronomic framework, bearing
its theological and didactic stamp. They are, in effect, illustrations written up from Israel's earlier experience, depicting lessons the writer wishes to present to his own age. The shape of
those lessons is evident from the observation that runs like a re-
frain through the entire book: the Israelites did what was evil
in the sight of the Lord, the Lord sold them into the hands of
their enemies who oppressed them for a given number of years.
Then they cried unto the Lord who raised up a savior who, in
turn, delivered them from the clutches of their enemies. So the
land had rest for a given number of years (cf. 2:11–17 and the
theological framework of each of the stories). More succinctly
put, this would be the sequence: disobedience—oppression—repentance—deliverance—rest.

The Judges and the Movements

The compiler draws upon historical movements to prove his
point. But one has the distinct impression that he is equally concerned with the functionaries around whom the several movements revolve. He calls them judges; their purpose is to free his
tribe or tribes from oppression. Hence he is also a savior or deliverer. The judge was not a law officer as such, though, with the
exception of Samson, he did render decisions at the city gate. He
was a charismatic, a spirit-filled person, one possessed of the
qualities of leadership. Nowadays we might refer to him as a
gifted person. What he was from the Israelite point of view is
best illustrated in Gideon who is described as one possessed of

pretty much alone with its problems; there was no general participation in any one of the movements. The nearest thing to it occurred in the Deborah-Barak onslaught against the Canaanite confederacy of Jabin and Sisera in which nearly all the tribes north of Benjamin participated. Many of the movements in Judges took place simultaneously.

The one controlling and unifying factor throughout the period was intense, even ferocious, loyalty to Israel's God as demonstrated by the daring military operations of the tribes and their leaders and the stirring Song of Deborah with its triumphant and invigorating theology.

When flowing locks were worn in Israel,
   When the people served freely, praise Yahweh!
Listen, O kings,
   Lend an ear, O rulers!
I to Yahweh,
   I will sing,
I will sing to Yahweh,
   The God of Israel!
O Yahweh, when you sallied forth from Seir,
   When you marched out of the land of Edom,
The earth convulsed,
   The heavens too reeled (even the clouds dropped water),
     The mountains shook,
Before Yahweh,
   The One of Sinai,
Before Yahweh,
   The God of Israel.
Awake, awake, Deborah,
   Awake, awake, sing a song!
Up, Barak,
   Seize your captives,
     Son of Abinoam!

Then let the survivor rule over the powerful,
  The people of Yahweh rule over the mighty!
. . . .
So, Yahweh, may all your enemies perish,
  But all your friends be like the rising sun (in his might).

(Judg. 5:2–5, 12–13, 31)

Yahweh of Israel was the Lord of hosts, a jealous God, present with his people when they were obedient to his will, righteous, ready and able to assist them in claiming the promise made to the fathers.

X

WE WANT A KING!
(I Samuel)

Given the relentless pressures exerted upon Israel from all sides and the corrosive immorality within, it is not surprising that the people requested a king (I Sam. 8:5-6). The external danger of Canaanism had been checked but the existence of local tribal enclaves with their peculiar attitudes and cultic practices proved even more ominous. Though the people of Baal were no longer a threat, the ideas and ways of Baal constituted a perennial peril that clung to the land like a thistle as may be seen from the sermons and complaints of the prophets. Yet the political forces pressing in upon strategic areas with such persistence were of more evident significance because they jeopardized the very existence of the Confederacy of Hebrew tribes.

The Samson stories (Judg. 13–16) reflect virtually complete Philistine domination in the low hill country. Their activity was stepped up during the Samuel period (about 1050–1020 B.C.). The first battle of Ebenezer (I Sam. 4) signalized a full invasion of Israel. Shiloh was destroyed, the Ark of the Covenant captured, and the High Priest's son slain (Ps. 78:60–64). Samuel filled the leadership vacuum and drove the invaders from their newly won position (I Sam. 7:10–14). But they did not remain inactive for long; they continued to plague the nation until the time of David. On the other side of the Jordan the Ammonites were not completely subdued by Jephthah. Hence, without some organization to weld all Israel into taking a concerted stand, survival might have been, to say the least, precarious.

Samuel

Samuel stands between the period of the Judges and that of the monarchy. He was not a member of a priestly family. There is a strong tradition voiced in a Dead Sea document,* Ecclesiasticus and the Mishnah to the effect that he was a Levite by dedication, that is, a Nazarite. The story of his upbringing at Shiloh (I Sam. 2–3) is well known. He learned more than the fine art of conducting rituals during his internship. He saw the needs of the people on the one hand and the growing corruption of the sons of Eli on the other. It was evident to him that the house of Eli could not minister effectively to the new and urgent situation.

Eli himself had been a good man in his day, but his day had ceased to be. Age and family difficulties rendered him unable to cope with the Philistine problem and with internal deterioration. After his death Samuel was catapulted into the position of power and responsibility. That he gained the respect of the Philistines after his successful resistance against them at Ebenezer is apparent from their permission for him to continue as judge, ruling his own people.

It was common practice in the ancient world for a local chief to be appointed by the dominant power. So far as the records

* 4QSam (col. 1, line 3) as published provisionally in BASOR 132 (December 1953), p. 26. The passage in question reads, "he shall be a *nazir* (nazarite) forever."

go, Samuel was thereafter occupied with the direction of Israel's internal affairs (I Sam. 7:15-17), the Philistines preferring his judgeship to less controllable local chieftains like Samson.

Although Samuel functioned as a judge, he cut loose from the official priests and became the founder of the prophetic movement. It is significant that the Ark of the Covenant remained at Kirjath-jearim all the days of Samuel and Saul. Neither it nor its priesthood figured in the conduct of the vital affairs of the day. Samuel was a prophet under direct call from the Lord and as such managed to hold Israel to the God of the fathers both in faith and life, taught them the fundamentals of covenant brotherhood, unified the tribes of the central highland, and so prepared them for the tasks ahead.

Saul

Samuel had the same troubles with his sons that bedeviled Eli with his. Moreover, another direction of leadership was required, one that could take advantage of the consolidations achieved by Samuel and at the same time meet aggressively the pressing political problems of the age. The real measure of Samuel's leadership was precisely the increasing popular dissatisfaction with it. The people were made aware of themselves because they were inspired with the zealous and vital faith in the God of the prophet-seer. In effect he succeeded in creating a degree of calm and confidence after the earlier rout of the Israelite army with its consequent loss of morale.

Then, too, as excavations all through the area and contemporary literature demonstrate, there was in the eleventh century a growing emphasis on commerce with concomitant expansion of the hegemony of merchant peoples, particularly along trade routes. From the east camel caravans bore their merchandise and

from the west pushed the Philistines, across the highways of Israel, to meet them. Amidst these commercial pressures it became
imperative for Israel to act to preserve its identity; perhaps some
of the more farsighted clan leaders saw an opportunity to capitalize on contemporary movements to their own advantage.

Several versions about the rise of Saul are current as may be
seen from a careful reading of I Samuel 9–15. But it seems clear
that the above described aspects of the situation played a major
role. Clearly a further step in the progress of Israel as God's
people was indicated. The leaders among the people approached
Samuel at Ramah with their request, "Make us a king to judge
(govern) us" (8:4–5). After divine consultation the old prophet
acceded. Possibly he was more cognizant of the position of his
people than they themselves were. Without some form of strong,
centralized organization they would be pulverized between the
millstones of Philistia and Ammon. Looking around they observed that Edom, Moab and Ammon were stable and prosperous by virtue of their virile leadership. All the surrounding
princedoms had an advanced degree of organization which enabled them to compete favorably in the growing trade interests
of the time and to hold their own in the struggle for power.

Saul was just the man to rally the forces of Israel. He was of
princely stature, the scion of a small tribe, without much prestige. Saul replied to Samuel who had invited him to eat with
him, "Am I not a Benjaminite, the smallest of the tribes of Israel, and my family the most insignificant in the tribe of Benjamin" (I Sam. 9:21). He had a deep feeling for Israel, as is
apparent from the vigorous action he took against Ammon in
defense of his Transjordan brethren (I Sam. 11) and the almost
continuous warfare against the persistent Philistines. Had he
maintained a healthy contact with Samuel and the prophet en-

thusiasts, he might have gone down in the history of Israel a greater personality than David. But he chose to revive the priestly house of Eli at Nob—a few miles south of Gibeah—possibly because of the rising tension between himself and the prophets and the fact that he could not go it alone in the religiously charged atmosphere of his time (I Sam. 21:1; 22:9, 11, 19).

Whatever may be one's final assessment of the character and place of Saul, he must give due weight to the true stature of the man and his leadership qualities. He checked the hostile pressures against Israel. In the battle of Gilboa in which he and Jonathan lost their lives and the army of Israel was ostensibly defeated, the Philistine grip on Israel was broken and the stage set for the more spectacular reign of David. Slowly and painfully, but no less certainly, God was establishing his people in the land to which he had led them (I Sam. 31).

XI

THE SON OF JESSE
(I Samuel 16–II Samuel 24)

Pride and a false sense of omniscience have conspired to wreck more than one personality in the course of history. They did so in the case of Saul. He had been an effective, sensitive exponent of the cause of Israel but eventually declared his independence of the prophets and lost touch with the people he had been chosen to serve. As on innumerable occasions later, God had to turn elsewhere for a leader-servant for his people. This time he would choose a man after his own heart (I Sam. 16:7).

So Samuel was sent to an out-of-the-way place in the hill country of Bethlehem, to a family of shepherds, to anoint a son of Jesse as successor to Saul. This time the choice fell upon the least likely of Jesse's sons, upon David, the youngest one who was busy tending the sheep—to the utter surprise of prophet and father, and probably to the consternation of the apparently more regal-looking brothers.

The Rise of David

The shepherd lad turned out to be a gifted personality; in fact he was the last of the charismatic leaders of Israel. Like Moses, he learned much in the pursuit of his task. Somehow, under the star-studded sky above Bethlehem's hills he imbibed a spirit of appreciation of the ways of God, came to understand his will, and developed an awareness of those qualities of devoted service displayed in his later life. There he acquired skills of leadership and the sense of dedication to God and duty that made him the man he was to be as king of Israel.

The rugged life in the hills generated sheer physical strength and agility. The more relaxed moments provided opportunity for thought and the cultivation of the soul so that the shepherd youth became an accomplished poet and musician. In due course, his fame spread through the neighborhood and he was summoned to the court of Saul as musician and attendant for the king. Many of the details of what transpired when he was in the service of Saul are reflections of an enthusiastic tradition, but the main outlines of the story of his rise in Israel are factual. Otherwise the conflict between him and the king are inexplicable. The latter could hardly help sensing in his young armorbearer and musician the very regal qualities he himself lacked, especially in the later years of his life.

When David was compelled to flee from the wrath of Saul, he sought the advice and help of Samuel (I Sam. 19:18–24). During his outlaw days he retained the affection of the crown prince, Jonathan, and was the recipient of many favors from him. That was, no doubt, due to Jonathan's recognition of the ability and character of David, and the latter's correct behavior toward him and his father. The days of outlawry never diminished the mutual respect of these young men for each other. David continued to grow in grace and power and gained further experience in leadership. Around him gathered a coterie of dissidents whom he welded into the most solidly loyal unit of supporters to be found anywhere in the history of the world. Despite numerous provocations to do otherwise, he always respected and protected the duly anointed king; he never engaged in any overt act of personal hostility or retaliation for the attempts upon his life. Even after he had been forced to seek refuge with the Philistines, he and his followers contrived to evade participation in their campaigns against his people.

David the King

Following the tragic defeat of Israel at Mount Gilboa (I Sam. 31), David appeared openly at Hebron, the capital of Judah (II Sam. 2), where his brethren installed him as king. Although intrigue was at work between some of his men and the erstwhile partisans of Saul, David took pains to avoid personal involvement. Meanwhile prosperity and progress smiled upon him and, after the death of Abner and Ishbaal, the elders of Israel journeyed to Hebron where they made a treaty with him and proclaimed him king also over Israel.

Naturally the growing power of David could not for long escape the attention of the Philistines whose vassal he still was, at least nominally. They took no action against him until his position grew to alarming proportions in the wake of the consolidation of the tribes of Israel under the man they had learned to respect and fear. When they did it was too late (II Sam. 5:17–25). Nevertheless David did not annex the Philistine country to Israel; he merely turned the table and made the Philistines vassals of his.

Secure against the old enemies of his people, David set about developing his rule by the establishment of a capital on a neutral site, outside the tribal system, at Jerusalem, the city of the Jebusites. Then he reclaimed the religious symbols neglected since the fall of Shiloh more than half a century before. He transferred the Ark of the Covenant to Jerusalem, reorganized the

cities of refuge, and, in all probability, arranged the regular func-
tioning of the priestly orders. In a word, David was responsible
for the amalgamation of the distraught religious elements of the
nation, providing for their service and control in the center of
authority. He always maintained close relationship with the
prophetic party represented by Nathan and Gad, the latter having joined him during his outlaw days.

David's achievements as king were, in no small measure, due
to his catering to the desires and prejudices of the people. He
took advantage of historical precedent by retaining the tribal system and by recruiting the traditional religious forces. In a sense
he pursued his ambition for Israel by playing on the harpstrings
of its very soul. He bound the heterogeneous tribal elements to
himself in a personal union rather than in an organizational one.
He wore the crown of Judah and the crown of Israel—never
that of an organizationally united kingdom of Israel.

As time went on, David came into collision with Moab and
Edom which were subdued and made tributary to him in a personal union. The Ammonite incident (II Sam. 10) occasioned
the reduction of the Aramaean states to the north and east, so
that the king's authority extended literally from Egypt to the
Euphrates (I Chron. 18:1–3). His was the mightiest empire in
the world of his time.

David the Man

David was one of the shrewdest politicians of all time. His desert
heritage taught him to deal diplomatically with every situation
that demanded his attention. He was a keen observer of human
nature and knew how to handle the most obstreperous characters
and win them to his support. Yet he was also quite human as
his family troubles and his affair with Bathsheba with its conse-

quences demonstrate. He was an intense personality as may be seen from the zeal displayed in every phase of his life activity. He was capable of inspiring tremendous loyalty but, on occasion, of arousing antipathy, as in the case of Sheba (II Sam. 20). He was a musician of note and a great poet. But perhaps most significantly, he was a profoundly religious person. He was a chief of sinners, yet when confronted by his sins he repented sincerely and honestly. He did not placate religious leaders or parties for purely political reasons. One cannot read the record without an acute awareness of the utter commitment of the man to what he believed to be the best religio-political policies for the nation.

XII

COURTING DISASTER
(I Kings 1–11)

Solomon may, in some respects, have been a wise man, but history does not certify him as being an astute and farsighted king. Under normal circumstances he would not have become king because he was not the eldest surviving son of David at the time. He owed his enthronement to a conspiracy of forces that operated in his favor and against that of Adonijah (I Kings 1).

In the case of Saul and David the choice was the Lord's, made through the prophets, with the consent of the people, and on the basis of the gift for leadership. Now, for the first time in Israel, dynastic succession as a principle became operative and was continued in the Southern Kingdom, without interruption, until its downfall in 587 B.C. An interesting fact is that both Zadok and Nathan—representatives of priesthood and prophecy—had a hand in the anointing ceremony (I Kings 1:45).

Reorganization of the Kingdom

Solomon began with a virtually clean state. Adonijah was soon put out of the way, Joab, David's commander was slain, and Abiathar, David's high priest, was retired to Anathoth. He offered some prospect for great things for the kingdom by deferring to his father's last requests with the promise of divine guid-

ance and blessing if he continued in obedience to the statutes
and commands of the Lord (I Kings 3:14). No sooner had he
stamped out effective opposition to himself than he proceeded
to strengthen his grip upon the helm of state (I Kings 4:1-6) by
the appointment of a cabinet to carry out his grandiose designs.

Lacking the personal qualities of leadership possessed by
David, he set to work forging a kingdom based on the principle
of absolute control enforced by a mailed fist. He saw to it that
the old personal loyalties so effective in the formation of his father's kingdom were dissolved. The venerable tribal system with
its local pride and prejudice was circumvented by the creation
of administrative districts that cut across tribal boundaries, governed by court officials and overseers, some of whom were directly related to the royal family (I Kings 4:7-19). These super-
visors displaced the unhappy tribal chiefs. The result was the
inauguration of a gigantic bureaucracy that sapped the strength
of the nation by its demands and ruthlessness (I Kings 4:22–
28). Perhaps the most heinous innovation was the institution of
the corvée, forced labor gangs, recruited from the various districts to serve in relays in carrying out Solomon's program of
kingdom glorification (I Kings 5:13-18).

Such an auspicious developmental policy testifies to the relative security of the land won by David. Archaeological surveys
and explorations in the central highland disclose burgeoning new
settlements springing up everywhere. Along with this went a
rapid increase of population and a corresponding growth in
wealth and prestige. Despite the corvée and heavy taxation comparative stability appears to have been maintained within the
original territorial limits of Israel. In outlying areas, however,
there were signs of growing restiveness. Hadad, the Edomite, rebelled (I Kings 11:14-22). So did Rezon of Damascus (I Kings

11:23–25). Inside Israel Jeroboam raised the standard of revolt (I Kings 11:26–40), though he failed to make much progress in the lifetime of Solomon. Nevertheless, the seeds of reaction were being sown; they sprouted and brought forth their bitter fruit in the years ahead. Solomon was master of Israel, but in the exercise of his hegemony he was flirting with disaster.

Solomon's Building Enterprises

One of the purposes of centralized control was the avoidance of internal troubles such as beset the last years of David's reign. But the paramount objective was preparation for the execution of the huge building program that required considerable labor and expense, both of which had to be provided by the common people. It is evident that in a country like Israel neither would be forthcoming without some pressure. To be sure David had accumulated much material and had outlined the plans for the Temple, but that could have been only a drop in the bucket of Solomon's immensely expanded building program. The construction enterprise carried out by Solomon was for Israel what that of the Fourth Dynasty with its colossal pyramids was for Egypt. Both nations had to be virtually enslaved by the ambitions of their rulers and were left bankrupt for many years.

According to the biblical story, Solomon's most auspicious projects consisted of the construction of a palace and Temple. Both could be accomplished only with the help of Phoenician experts who supervised the work (I Kings 7; II Chron. 2). They furnished Lebanese cedar for paneling and other decorative work, fashioned the precious metals for the ornaments, and assisted in the quarrying and dressing of the stones.

The palace was actually the more elaborate and costly of the two structures, and took twice as long to build (I Kings 6:37–

7:1). It was nearly twice (150 × 75 × 45 feet) the size of the Temple (90 × 30 × 45 feet), which was probably a royal chapel attached to the palace as was the practice in Assyria. The palace was about the size of two average building lots in a small town or city; the Temple was about as large as an average-size barn on one of our better farms. If both buildings were in process simultaneously the work occupied a third of Solomon's reign; if consecutively half of it.

Those structures alone would have been sufficient to immortalize their builder. But they were only a portion of his achievements (I Kings 9:15–19). At Elath, on the Gulf of Aqabah, he built a huge seaport, with ample storage facilities, and a fleet (I Kings 9:26–28) that plowed the seas to Ophir whence they brought gold, spices, sandalwood, ivory and monkeys. He rebuilt the city of Gerar, fortified Gezer, erected housing for his horses and chariots at Megiddo, Tell el-Hesi, Hazor, Gezer and Taanach. At Megiddo alone there was room for stabling about 300 horses, which makes the reference to his horses and chariots in I Kings 10:26 not too extravagant.

Solomon's wealth and glory paraded before the Queen of Sheba, who had come to Jerusalem on a diplomatic mission, was no exaggeration as excavations of contemporary city levels in Palestine prove.

> The Queen of Sheba, made fully aware of all the wisdom of Solomon, the palace he had built, his table fare, the seating arrangement of his courtiers, his butlers, and the burnt offerings he was accustomed to offer in the temple of Yahweh, was breathless. . . . Solomon received around twenty million dollars worth of gold annually, apart from what accrued from mercantile taxes and increments from trade with Arab kings and from local governors. . . . King Solomon surpassed all the kings of the earth in wealth and wisdom. The entire world

conferred with Solomon to benefit from the wisdom with which God had blessed him. Each one brought his tribute—vessels of silver and gold, robes, spices, horses and mules—a fixed quantity every year. Solomon also obtained chariots and horses—he quartered fourteen hundred chariots and twelve thousand horses in chariot cities or in Jerusalem with the king. The king made silver as trivial as stones in Jerusalem, and cedar as abundant as sycamores in the Shephelah. Solomon's horses were imported from Cilicia; the crown agents imported them from Cilicia at prevalent prices—an Egyptian chariot for about four hundred dollars in silver and a Cilician horse for about a hundred dollars in silver—and delivered them at that rate through their agency to all the Hittite and Syrian kings.

(I Kings 10:4, 5, 14-15, 23-29)

Next to Herod the Great, Solomon was the greatest Jewish builder.

Other Projects and Estimate

In addition to his building operations, but equally significant, were the king's other exploits. He was a great merchant prince engaged in all sorts of mercantile activity. He imported chariots from Egypt which he delivered to the Hittite and Aramaean kings and provided Cilician horses for his customers (I Kings 10:28-29). He negotiated commercial agreements with southern Arabian rulers (I Kings 10:14-15). His Red Sea fleet was, of course, established for trade.

Activities of such a character required all kinds of arrangements, including alliances and treaties guaranteed by marriages to foreign princesses which, in turn, necessitated provision for their living accommodations and religious practices. Naturally those expedients led to dangerous domestic relations, not the least of which was the creation of an atmosphere of religious compromise for which he was severely condemned.

In addition to Pharaoh's daughter, King Solomon took in
marriage many foreign women—Moabites, Ammonites, Edomites, Sidonians and Hittites—from the very nations against
which Yahweh had warned the Israelites: "You must not con-
sort with them nor they with you, because they will certainly
turn your affections to their gods." Nevertheless, Solomon became fondly attached to them. He had seven hundred wives
and three hundred concubines who misled him. When Solomon grew older, they converted him to other gods and he no
longer remained true to Yahweh his God, as David his father
did. Solomon became a follower of Ashtoreth, the goddess of
the Sidonians, and of Milcom, the abomination of the Ammonites. . . . Solomon even erected a high place on the hill in
front of Jerusalem for Chemosh, the abomination of Moab, and
for Milcom, the abomination of the Ammonites. Thus Solomon
made provision for all his pagan wives who burned incense and
sacrificed to their gods.   (I Kings 11:1–5, 7–8)

Despite his early good intentions to glorify God and Israel, it
can, without misrepresentation, be said that Solomon ignited
the flames of political and religious disaster. The latter did not
come until much later, in the days of Josiah. The former befell
the kingdom almost immediately, under his successor. Solomon's
kingdom rested on the flimsy foundations of material progress
in economics, politics and religion. Its glory was like the bril-
liance of the setting sun, the harbinger of descending darkness
and gloom.

XIII

THE END OF THE BEGINNING
(I Kings 12:1–24, 14:21–31)

The history of Israel from the time of Moses to Solomon, sometimes a bit checkered, was, on the whole, progressive and il-
lustrious. The former had fused the motley tribes into a semblance of unity. Under Joshua the twelve-tribe amphictyony was
centered about the Shiloh shrine. After its destruction by the
Philistines, the feeling for covenantal brotherhood was maintained by the prophet Samuel on the one hand, and on the other
by the popular response to the challenge to Israel's very existence
by external pressures from almost every side. The people's faith
in themselves as God's chosen people, and the courage and vigor
born of that faith, enabled them to outwit or overcome all the
adversities that threatened them. So long as the choice of leader
was God's and he, in turn, remained loyal to the covenant with
all its traditions, the nation continued to grow in strength and
purpose.

In the later years of David, however, events took another turn.
Rebellion raised its head, family troubles marred the early pattern of success, and the pride of material achievement exempli-
fied by the building plans of the old king began to gnaw away
the sinews of the erstwhile tranquil relationship between royalty
and people. When Solomon became king, he set about making a

name for himself. Henceforth the watchword was "Solomon in all his glory" while the covenant of brothers was displaced by the corvée, the enslavement of brothers. What a marvelous prospect appeared for Israel in the Davidic empire! But Solomon's kingdom marked the beginning of the end of what was left of the tribal union; it paved the way for ruin. Perhaps the way of empire was not for Israel, the people of God.

Which Way Israel?

It is no accident that prophecy was virtually quiescent during the reign of Solomon. He had seized control of religion, as may be seen from his innovations, attempting to update the whole worship system by patterning it after that of the Canaanites. Why then, did Rehoboam repair to Shechem for his formal investiture (I Kings 12:1)?

Shechem was the old cult center where Joshua bade farewell to Israel in a final covenant ceremony (Josh. 24) and, in all probability, a periodic covenant-renewal rite took place there (cf. Deut. 11:26–32; 27:1–26). That being the case, Rehoboam journeyed to Shechem at the beginning of his reign to participate in the traditional observance so charged with meaning for the people. Such an act was fraught with special significance at the time for both the king and his subjects.

In harmony with the occasion, the new king was presented with a bill of particulars—grievances for whose redress the people petitioned. They could no longer submit to the heavy yoke of taxation or endure the forced labor Solomon had imposed upon them without their consent. Hence they availed themselves of the prerogative their fathers exercised in connection with the appointment of Saul and David, they claimed a voice in the direction of kingdom affairs by demanding a covenant of stipulations from Rehoboam.

Stunned by their ultimatum, the king requested three days time to consult his advisers. The implications were unmistakable —constitutional versus absolute monarchy, the direction taken by Solomon. The seasoned politicians advised a return to the line followed by David (I Kings 12:7). The inexperienced officials belonging to the king's own coterie counseled continuation and strengthening the policies of his father (I Kings 12:10–11). It was only natural for the youthful monarch, encouraged by the overwhelmingly enthusiastic advice of his friends, to reject the popular plea and the suggestions of the elders. He doubtless had visions of grandeur, of adding to the glory of Solomon and of making Israel even more splendorous.

Popular Reaction

Rehoboam had it in his power to become a second David, but he made the wrong choice, on the spur of the moment and without the slightest consideration for the aggrieved. He brushed aside with contempt the old covenant tradition. The result was the precipitate end of the roseate beginning under David. The northern tribes helped to bring David's earlier ambition to fruition; they now proceeded to deal in their own way with his overzealous grandson. The ditty of I Kings 12:16 tells the story in a nutshell.

> What portion have we in David?
> We have no inheritance in the son of Jesse.
> To your tents, O Israel!
> Look, now, after your own house, O David.

Jeroboam, who had taken exception to Solomon's corvée (I Kings 11:26–40), was summoned from exile in Egypt to assume leadership of the old northern Tribal Confederation. In the meantime Rehoboam was wisely dissuaded (I Kings 12:21–24) from resorting to military action against the rebels and chose to be content with the territory left to him. He retained the royal establishment at Jerusalem with its bureaucracy but lacked the revenue to support it.

Although it is futile to speculate on what might have been if conditions had been otherwise, it is certain that if Solomon and his successor had been less concerned about the glory of the nation and more about the divine covenant with its emphasis upon brotherhood and the welfare of the people, the course of Israel's history would have been different. With the advent of Jeroboam and the consequent division of the Solomonic kingdom came internal weakness and dissension which laid open all the territory of Israel to foreign exploitation. In its wake came the invasion of Shishak (ca. 935–914 B.C.), the first king of the twenty-second Egyptian dynasty (I Kings 14:25–26) who took Jerusalem, rifled the Temple and its treasury (in the fifth year of Rehoboam, ca. 917 B.C.). According to his inscription in the Temple of Amun at Karnak, his army overran more than fifty cities of Israel and close to a hundred in Judah (cf. II Chron. 12:4). He set up a victory stele at Meggido which was uncovered some years ago by the University of Chicago expedition. Whether the Pharaoh was called in by Jeroboam or took advantage of the situation on his own initiative is unknown. But his victory accentuates the rapidity of the deterioration after Rehoboam's fateful decision.

Further Developments

Several new movements now took place. First, the Chronicler informs us that Rehoboam strengthened the defenses of Jerusalem and fortified the cities on the border and interior of Judah after the Egyptian foray (II Chron. 11:5–12). He placed his own sons or relatives in charge of them (II Chron. 11:23)—a practice inaugurated by his father. That was like locking the door after the horse was stolen. No amount of political maneuvering or military preparation could undo the damage done by the king's decision and Shishak's invasion. A more hopeful outcome was the increasing activity of prophets. In Judah Shemaiah took a hand in the affairs of the day (I Kings 12:21–24); in Israel Ahijah of Shiloh proclaimed the word of the Lord to the king (I Kings 14:1–18). Thus it was that prophecy began to assume its henceforth ever-present role as critic of king and institutional religion which almost always supported him. And so

> The moving finger writes; and, having writ,
> Moves on; nor all thy piety nor wit
> Shall lure it back to cancel half a line,
> Nor all thy tears wash out a word of it.*

* Omar Khayyam, *Rubaiyat*, Stanza 71.

A CHAMPION FOR THE LORD
(I Kings 17–21, II Kings 1)

The problems besetting both kingdoms after the schism called forth the most dynamic religious movement in the history of the Hebrew people. It arose almost spontaneously and, for the most part, could not be controlled by priestly or royal officialdom. It manifested an independence not apparent in the official cult which doubtless had its own corps of prophets. The great prophets owed their position to membership in the intimate Council of the Lord* (cf. Jer. 23:18–22); they were fiercely loyal to him as Lord of heaven and earth. The prophets of the Golden Age (i.e., the period of the pre-writing prophets) were men of deeds, in themselves the divine fiat upholding the covenant of the Lord.

When they appeared the nation seemed to be pretty well off, religiously speaking. At Jerusalem the Temple was in operation and, with few exceptions, was fulfilling its function. We do read about cleansings or cult reformations, but that was not because

---

* The intimate Council of Yahweh refers to the celestial court in which the true prophets conceived themselves as being present, hearing his word, and being informed of his decisions and message for the people. The best illustrations of the heavenly court are to be found in Job 1 and 2, and Isaiah 6:1–13.

of indifference to religion. It was rather because all sorts of bar-
nacles had attached themselves to the temple cult. In the north
Jeroboam had erected two centers for worship—one at Bethel,
the other at Dan. There the great champion of the Lord performed his mighty acts in the second quarter of the ninth century B.C.

Religious Development in Israel

Jeroboam did what any ruler might have been expected to do:
he provided worship centers for his people to prevent their going to Jerusalem and possibly defecting to Judah (I Kings 12:
27). In so doing he catered to the more conservative tradition of
Israel—giving official status to the shrine at Dan (Judg. 18)
and reviving the old high place at Bethel (= house of God),
an ancient cult center as excavations have shown. He unified
the pattern of religion in his kingdom by the symbol of the
Golden Calf which eventually became a snare to the people.
I Kings 13–14 indicates that there was some opposition to Jeroboam's cult, but it was soon diverted to another direction. The
golden calves were, as a matter of fact, not idols; they were
pedestals* for the invisible presence of the Lord, just as the Ark
of the Covenant at Jerusalem was regarded as his throne. They
did, however, offer suggestiveness in that direction when their

* The function of the bulls as pedestals is confirmed from numerous
iconographic representations from Palestine and Syria. The gods of
the Hittites, Canaanites and Aramaeans are frequently depicted
standing on animals. For illustrations see *Arslan Tash* by F. Thu-
reau-Dangin, A. Barrois, G. Dossin, M. Dunand (Paris, 1931): Atlas,
Plate II, No. 1; *Orientalia*, Vol. 15 (1946), pp. 1–45 and plates;
Vol. 18 (1949), Plate 28; *The Hittites* by O. R. Gurney (Baltimore,
1952), p. 137.

significance was forgotten and because they were always visible to the worshipers, as the Ark was not.

Israel thus became a self-sufficient entity with its religious and political institutions. Nevertheless, its geographical location made it susceptible to external influences which were encouraged by the ambition of its kings to obviate the loss of the prestige of Jerusalem. Trade and commerce with surrounding nations flourished as may be seen from the excavations at Samaria. One of the prime examples of foreign relationships is that of the marriage of Ahab to Jezebel, the daughter of the priest-king Ethbaal of Tyre-Sidon.

From Israel's side it was propaganda. The Tyrian princess was a devout follower of Asherah whose cult she introduced into Israel and supported with vigor (cf. I Kings 18:19). In the Ugaritic texts discovered at Ras Shamra, on the North Syrian coast, Asherah is regarded as the wife of the great god El, the head of the pantheon. She is referred to as Asherah of the Sea and later became the chief goddess of Tyre where she was associated with Baal. As such both Baal and Asherah were introduced into Samaria by Jezebel. It is possible that Ethbaal had married another of his daughters to Bir-Hadad of Damascus who was won over to the religion of Baal-Melkart to whom he dedicated a stele found some years ago near Aleppo.

Religious Conflict in Israel

Kings before Ahab are accused of defection from the statutes and judgments of the Lord but none more severely castigated for apostasy than the son of Omri. A portentous threat hung over the nation due to the influx of Tyrian Baalism with its evident subversion of the religion of many of its citizens. The beliefs and practices of Baalism may be judged by the performance of its priests at Mount Carmel (I Kings 18:26–29) and Jezebel's handling of the Naboth vineyard case (I Kings 21:1–14). It was orgiastic in expression, licentious in character, lacking in morality, and utterly contemptuous of Israelite ancestral traditions.

Just when Israel's religious skies were darkest, arose a champion for the Lord. Like the rising of a star out of the eastern desert came the rugged personality from Tishbe in Gilead. He bore the confessional name of Elijah (Yahweh is my God). He was called by the Lord to present the nation with a fateful choice. Despite all the regular and special fertility rituals celebrated in honor of Baal, a supposedly agricultural deity, the land remained in the grip of a stubborn drought. To break it, Elijah intervened by calling for a confrontation between the God of Israel and Baal on Mount Carmel, the most sacred of the latter's sanctuaries. Really more was at stake now than in the contest between the Lord and the Pharaoh. The way of Baal was more insidious than that of the god of Egypt, and hence more dangerous. Baal claimed to be a cosmic deity, lord of heaven and earth, which was precisely what the Lord was considered to be by his adherents. But there could not be two cosmic deities, as Elijah affirmed in his famous challenge hurled at the worshipers on Carmel that day: "If Yahweh is God, follow him, but if Baal (is god), follow him" (I Kings 18:21).

The issue involved in the Mount Carmel struggle was between Yahweh, beside whom there was no other god, and Baal-Melkart whom Jezebel and her followers regarded as lord of heaven and earth. It was not simply one between Yahweh, the God of Israel, and Baal, a local fertility deity. The personalities participating in the contest were devotees of deities both of whom claimed cosmic power. Now both parties could not be right; one must be wrong. It is precisely because of the nature of the claims put forth between Elijah on the one hand, and the prophets of Baal on the other, that the Yahweh-Baal contest assumed such an important role in the religious history of Israel.

The outcome of the contest was a defeat for Baal on his own ground. Popular reaction was instantaneous: "Yahweh is God, Yahweh is God" (I Kings 18:39), they shouted. The devotees of Baal were dealt with in the manner of the time and, while Baalism was not finally rooted out at once, its back was broken.

Jezebel, angered by the destruction of the prophets of Baal, vowed to do away with Elijah. The latter fled to Mount Horeb (I Kings 19), an old cultic center of Israel, where he was renewed in faith and inspired to take advantage of the unstable political situation to work the way of the Lord. Yahweh was Lord of nations and would implement his will partly through the interplay of international forces and partly through the continuity of prophecy. So he was directed to anoint Hazael as king of Syria and Elisha as his own successor.

However, before these acts of the prophet could bear fruit, Elijah was to have another brush with the royal house. This time it was in connection with the Naboth vineyard incident in which was reflected one of the most detestable ways of Canaan—that of commercialism. Theoretically, land in Israel could not be sold; it belonged to the Lord (Ps. 24:1). The ancient patrimony was always regarded as sacred. That was why Naboth refused to sell his vineyard to Ahab. Jezebel's intervention, heedless of the way of Israel and by wholly unjust means, brought down upon her and the Omri dynasty the wrath of the old prophet. He announced its downfall and the horrible fate of the queen.

For Jezebel the end justified the means. Ahab wanted Naboth's vineyard which the latter refused to sell to the king by virtue of patrimonial obligations (cf. Lev. 25:23–28; Num.

36:7; Jer. 32:7–10)—the law specified that land could not be sold in perpetuity because it was the gift of Yahweh, first to the tribes of Israel, then to the families within the tribes. In fact one could not, theoretically, sell land at all, only the usufruct. The queen was brought up in a very different atmosphere—that of Phoenicia—where the commercial principle applied to land as well as to chattels. Hence she had no feeling for the Israelite way. Moreover, she was a devotee of the Tyrian gods, Baal and Asherah, who were an immoral and licentious pair, with no sense of truthfulness and honesty, righteousness and covenant. That is why she could nonchalantly arrange for the judicial murder of Naboth on the basis of false testimony given by acknowledged scoundrels (I Kings 21:10).

After the death of Naboth, Ahab went to claim the vineyard where he was accosted by Elijah. Seeing him, the king exclaimed, "Have you found me, O my enemy?"

"I have indeed," the prophet retorted. "I have found you and because you have resolved to do evil in the sight of Yahweh I am about to bring disaster upon you; I will wipe you out completely, and cut off, without exception, all Ahab's male issue in Israel. I will make your house like that of Jeroboam the son of Nebat, and like that of Baasha the son of Ahijah, because you have provoked me and led Israel to sin. Moreover, of Jezebel has Yahweh said, 'The dogs will devour Jezebel in the valley of Jezreel . . . and Ahab's dead in the city, and the dead in the field will the birds of the heavens consume'" (I Kings 21:20–24).

By virtue of his adherence to stern desert justice, unswerving loyalty to the Lord, and unremitting zeal for the true religion of Israel Elijah stands out as the Old Testament representative of prophecy and, as such, appeared with Moses on the mount of the transfiguration (Matt. 17:1–13).

A NIAGARA OF RIGHTEOUSNESS
(Amos)

The Old Testament is the most practical library ever assembled. So often it is viewed, mistakenly I think, as a lawbook full of awesome and irrelevant regulations that tend to hinder rather than to promote the free exercise of one's faith. It is a book of life, everyday life at that. That is what makes it so interesting and applicable to life situations today and why the reader must visualize the living, throbbing milieu out of which it came.

Nothing could be plainer or more intelligible than the basic thrust of the sermons of prophets when they are understood in the light of the historical context. The prophets were concerned with local conditions, problems and crises. In effect they were God's word in the history of their times. Old Testament revelation was, therefore, largely directional in character, offering guidance and counsel for the people of the Lord in the midst of all sorts of exigencies and circumstances.

The Times

The first of the writing prophets, Amos, was summoned to service sometime in the reign of Jeroboam II (786–746 B.C.), when Israel was enjoying a veritable Indian summer. The reigns of his immediate predecessors were occupied almost continuously

in wars with Syria. When Adad-nirari III (810–783 B.C.) as-
cended the throne of Assyria, some of the Aramaean states revolted and joined in an attack upon Hamath, an act that brought
swift reprisal from him. He smashed the coalition and conducted
a full-fledged expedition against Damascus. No sooner was that
kingdom humbled than trouble brewed elsewhere which required
his immediate attention. With Damascus weakened and the Assyrian monarch busy mending the disintegrating seams of his
empire, Jehoash (801–786 B.C.) retook the cities wrested from
Israel earlier (II Kings 13:25). His son was able to extend the
hegemony of Israel almost to the northern limits of the old
Davidic kingdom (II Kings 14:25). Such sweeping power with
its control of the trade routes and consequent internal prosperity
was accompanied by luxurious living, popular and national
pride, and religious self-satisfaction. All oriental religions assumed that prosperity and success was indicative of divine favor
and blessing. Israel was a party to the same notion.

The prosperity equals divine approval equation had a profound effect upon the religious ideas and practices of the day.
Though not much is said about them in the book of Kings, a
great deal is revealed in the book of Amos. For one thing there
was no lack of formal religion, what has been referred to as re-
ligion-on-parade. Sacrifices were offered daily, tithing was practiced beyond the requirements of the Law (Amos 4:4d; cf. Deut.
14:28; 26:12; Num. 18:21–28), and freewill offerings were presented with pomp and ceremony (Amos 4:5). Feasts and festivals were observed, perhaps extra ones invented to make doubly
sure of the continuity of the divine gifts they thought they were
deservedly enjoying (5:21, 22, 25). There was loose talk about
the Day of the Lord (5:18–20) which many believed was about
to dawn, a day of light and brightness, and endless enjoyment

of placid material prosperity at home and dominion over other nations. Dedication vows were ridiculed and local prophets forbidden to speak (2:11), possibly persecuted.

The Man

Meanwhile, in the stern and rugged wilderness school of Tekoa, God was preparing one of his greatest prophets. There Amos learned the severe, often unattractive lessons of life. Somehow God seems to have been much closer to the herdsman in his adverse surroundings than he was to the churchgoers of Bethel. To Amos he disclosed himself as the covenant God who delighted in right, a God concerned about human values. He taught the prophet the importance of hard work, of obedience, of responsibility, and of the inexorable principle of equivalent compensation. Nature was niggardly in his country which apparently wouldn't even support the ordinary kind of sheep. The sycamore fruit required special treatment for early ripening to provide sustenance over a longer period.

Except for the divine presence, the wind-swept, stony hills around Tekoa were a lonely place. Natives could wander about for days without meeting, except by appointment. Wild beasts infested the countryside. Birds were few. The brilliantly radiant stars must have been a subject for contemplation on more than one occasion. The rough, stony ground, the precipitous hillsides, the barren soil were Amos' ever-present companions. No wonder he thundered against the profligate and self-indulgent pleasures afforded by the more propitious land to the north.

The Message

At the time of our prophet there was no tension between Israel and Judah. Indeed some scholars believe there was co-operation between Jeroboam II and Uzziah (Azariah).* In any event, there was no difficulty in going from one kingdom to the other as the sudden appearance of Amos at Bethel proves. He may have been on a kind of trade mission, offering some of the produce of patch and range for sale to the more prosperous and wealthy residents of the northern cities.

His arrival coincided, deliberately so, with a religious festival. That was when people from all over the land gathered at the shrine in holiday mood, worshiped and joined in fellowship, and when tinkers and itinerants peddled their wares. On the surface it looked quite proper. A people so manifestly blessed ought to present thank offerings to the Lord. Yet the tragedy was that they were less than expressions of genuine devotion to the Lord. The religion of this people was like a garment that could be put on or off as occasion demanded. All Israelites were brethren but Amos soon found out that their lives failed to support that fact. They were interested in keeping those aspects of the Torah that suited their convenience. Theirs was but token worship. The poor were sold into slavery for a token payment to make the transaction legal, the rights of the needy trampled upon, fathers entered into fraudulent agreements and sons swore to their valid- ity, garments taken in pledge, instead of being returned accord- ing to law (Ex. 22:26), were used in the religion of brotherhood for carousal, debauchery and pagan-like fertility rites. Thus said the Lord:

* So-called in II Kings. Kings of Judah sometimes bore two names, given names and throne names. For instance, Solomon's given name was Jedidiah (II Sam. 12:25), Jehoiakim's was Eliakim (II Kings 23:34), Zedekiah's was Mattaniah (II Kings 24:17). Azariah = Yahweh has helped; Uzziah = Yahweh is my strength or refuge.

For three outrages of Israel
  and for four,
I cannot avert judgment.
Because they sell an honest man for money
And a poor man for as little as a pair of sandals:
They trample on the head of the helpless,*
They twist the way of the humble.**

A man and his father act in collusion,
  in thus desecrating my holy name.

Upon pledged garments they stretch out
  alongside of every altar,
  and the wine of the fined
  they swill in their temple.   (2:6–8)

Such bankrupt, deceptive religion could not be condoned by
the herdsman-prophet whom the Lord, by his present observations, had aroused to be his spokesman. Through all his pronouncements of the word of the Lord runs, like a silver thread,
the demand for righteousness in life, as becomes the elect of the
Lord. Righteousness, as Johannes Pedersen and others have
pointed out, does not mean conformity to a code. Only two
terms generally designating legal precepts occur in Amos (*torah*
and statute) and they appear in a passage which was probably inserted into the book later (2:4–5). It means basically to act according to the nature of one's soul or being which, for Israel,
exists only by virtue of the covenant of the Lord. What Amos
calls for is that the religious devotees of the nation live and act
toward one another in harmony with their covenanted faith, in

* I.e., ride roughshod over them, trampling them down upon the dust
of the earth.
** I.e., make difficult the life of the meek.

accordance with the nature of their existence (sons of the covenant) as the people of God. That required treating one another as brothers, not as chattels. The only salvation for Israel as a nation now would be a veritable Niagara of righteousness with its concomitant expression in brotherhood.

> Let justice (at the gate) roll on like floodwaters,
> Righteousness like a never-failing stream.
>
> (5:24)

XVI

COVENANT LOVE
(Hosea)

The prophets were always situation preachers. They proclaimed the word of God at a specific time, in a specific environment, and with reference to a specific problem. They received the word in or became the word of the Lord to the people of their age who were plagued by a particular sin against him or who deviated from his covenant. Called by the Lord as his mouthpiece and yet being one of the people, they exhibited peculiar personal tendencies and traits that colored the attitude of their messages. Thus the rugged personality of Amos developed in the austere surroundings of Tekoa determined to some degree the character of his sermons on the righteousness of God.

Hosea

Hosea was a very different person and much closer to the people to whom he was charged to bring the word of the Lord. The worm of prosperity so evident in the pronouncements of his older contemporary was beginning to turn. The onslaughts of Assyria against the west under Tiglath-pileser III (745–727 B.C.) with their dire consequences for Israel had begun. The outward stability of the kingdom under Jeroboam II had given way to virtual anarchy. His successor, Zechariah, had ruled for only six months (II Kings 15:8), when upstart Shallum conspired against him and slew him (II Kings 15:10). A month later Shallum himself met a similar fate (II Kings 15:13) at the hands of Menahem (745–738 B.C.), who was soon brought under Assyrian vassalage in the wake of the reorganization of that empire. There was to be no more peace and tranquillity for Israel (II Kings 15:23–30; 17:1–6). From 746 to 722 B.C. Israel had six kings, a clear indication of her internal instability.

That was the atmosphere in which Hosea lived. John S. Sargent's masterly Frieze of the Prophets in the Boston Public Library portrays Hosea as a subdued young man, with keen insight, to be sure, but overwhelmed by a pathos brought on, in part, by the self-degradation of his fellow countrymen. The chapters of his book tell us precisely why the prophet felt as he did and why he addressed Israel in such sympathetic terms.

He was a family man and his experience as such illustrates the intimate relationship between the Lord and his people. He married, he says, a woman of harlotries; that is, a woman who was part of the harlotrous nation. She was not a harlot when he married her. Of this marriage were born children given names symbolic of judgment: Jezreel, the place of judgment; Unloved, the judgment cause; Not-my-people, the direction of judgment. Then, apparently, Hosea suffered the personal tragedy the Lord had undergone with his people. Nevertheless, he could not bring himself to divorce his wife. Despite her adultery, he continued to love her and could not let her go. So he decided to seek her out and win her back to himself. Hence it is that under the figure of a lover endeavoring to reclaim his wayward wife, Hosea presents the covenant love of the Lord going out to deliver Israel from perishing in the desert of religious harlotry.

Israel's Spurning of Covenant Love

Like all the other prophets, Hosea views the covenant tradition as basic in the relationship between the Lord and Israel. The Lord never violated the covenant. Israel's history is studded with defection, rejection and outright dereliction. Though the actual word for covenant occurs only five times therein, the sermons of Hosea are full of covenant terminology. The two most prominent terms involved are love (found nineteen times) and *hesed* (= steadfast love, covenant love, loyalty, devotion), occurring some six times in crucial passages.

Hosea's complaint, simply stated, is that Israel has played the harlot and exchanged her love for the Lord for shame (Hos. 4:7b). It is no accident that she is likened to a harlot who has spurned legitimate love for wantonness, has committed whoredom against him who was her first love, who wooed her in the wilderness and whom she was eager to follow when the going was tough. In the course of later life, in the glorious days of Jeroboam II, she forgot her earlier plight and became religiously sensual. That meant that she had really fractured her covenant love with the Lord, though she still occupied his land.

No outward semblance, however, could cover up the realities of the situation. There was "no faithfulness, no covenant love, no knowledge of God" (4:1). The very guiding principles of life, so graciously given and so auspiciously received at Sinai, were nullified by her prostitutions. There was "cursing, lying, murder, theft, adultery, and crime upon crime" (4:2)—note that the terminology here is nearly the same as that in the Decalogue. The roots of the words for murder, theft and adultery are exactly the same as in the Ten Commandments. Religious devotees may have thought they were worshiping the Lord, but if that was the case they were doing it by the way of Baal. In effect they had lost their faculty of discernment and discrimination, and continuance in aberrations could only lead to utter ruin (4:14e). No appeal to or alliance with foreign political leaders could save them or their land (5:13–14). Their salvation could come only from the Lord, though even he could not deliver them if they failed to respond to his covenant love.

The Seeking Love of God

As Jesus taught us (Luke 20:9–16), the Lord is not easily discouraged. He never deserts his children, though they may forsake him. That was, in a nutshell, the message of Hosea. As he loved his wife and would never leave her to her paramours who sought only to gratify their own pleasures, so the Lord would never leave off loving and wooing his sons and daughters.

"I will lure her away, bring her to the wilderness and speak to her heart" (2:14 = 2:16 in the Hebrew text), and make "the Valley of Achor (= trouble; cf. Josh. 7:26) a gate of hope" (2:15 = 2:17 in Heb. text).

If she responds, Jezreel will become a fruit-bearing plain instead of a battlefield, the Unloved will become the Beloved, and Not-my-people will become My-people (2:23 = 2:25 in Heb. text).

The Lord God of Hosea, as portrayed in Marc Connelly's *The Green Pastures* ([New York, 1935], Part II, Scenes 7 and 8), is vitally concerned about his people. Nowhere, except in the cross of our Saviour, do we see the profound pathos and compassion of the Lord expressed so vividly as in the following lamentation:

When Israel was a youth, I came to love him,
And from Egypt I summoned his sons.

The more I appealed to them,
The more they deserted me.
To Baal they sacrificed,
To images they burned incense.
I taught Ephraim to walk,
I lifted them up in my arms;
But they did not know that I bound up their wounds.
With human lines I led them,
With cords of love.
I was to them like those who raise the suckling to their cheeks,
I bent down to them and fed them.
. . . .
How can I abandon you, Ephraim, hand you over, Israel?
How can I deal with you like Admah, make you like Zeboiim?
My heart revolts against me,
My love is deeply stirred.
I cannot give vent to my great anger,
I cannot again destroy Ephraim,
For I am God, not man,
The Holy One in your midst.   (11:1-4, 8-9)

What a wonderful picture of the covenant love of the Lord for
Israel.

XVII

A HOLY GOD
(Isaiah 1–39)

Each of the prophets developed a peculiar theme of teaching that more than any other characterized his message which was consonant with his experience and apropos to the situation he faced. Amos was the prophet of righteousness, Hosea of covenant love, and Jeremiah of the inner life or the new covenant. Isaiah stressed the qualities of holiness and faithfulness as those aspects of human response to God most essential for his day. That does not mean that others were neglected or unemployed. For example, the root for righteousness appears twenty-nine times in his writings, that for judgment twenty-two times. He has something to say about the Torah, the divine favor, and the statutes of the law.

A Prophet of Judah

Isaiah was the first of the writing prophets of Judah. His prophecy, according to the superscription, spanned the reigns of four kings. His prophetic career, however, could hardly have begun before the end of the reign of Uzziah who died in 742 B.C. Neither could it have covered more than half of that of Hezekiah. The last clear historical testimony connects him with the invasion of Sennacherib in 701 B.C. (37:21; II Kings 19:6–7). The historical situation that called forth his initial prophecies was the westward surge of the Assyrians.

The first contact between Assyria and Judah came in the reign of Ahaz (735–715 B.C.) who, when threatened by a coalition composed of Syria and Israel attempting to force him into an ill-advised alliance of western kinglets against the powerful Tiglath-pileser III, purchased the latter's intervention (II Kings 16:5–9). Isaiah was bitterly opposed to Ahaz's course of action, knowing full well that it entailed vassalage to Assyria which, in turn, involved religious subservience. He directed his most pointed and severe barbs against Ahaz, as may be seen from the Immanuel prophecy of 7:10–17. Upon Ahaz's refusal of the prophet's proffered sign as a warning against becoming involved in the confused world political situation, Isaiah proceeded to deliver Yahweh's own sign:

> Listen now, O house of David! Is it too slight a matter for you to harass men, that you must harass my God too? There-fore, the Lord himself will provide for you a sign: Look, the maiden is pregnant and shall bear a son and name him Im-manuel (= God with us). He shall eat butter and honey be-fore he knows how to reject evil and choose good, for before the lad knows how to reject evil and choose good the land be-fore whose two kings you cringe shall be forsaken. Yahweh will bring upon you and your people and upon the house of your father such times as have not been since the time that Ephraim was separated from Judah—no less than the king of Assyria.
>
> (Is. 7:13–17)

The immediate implication of that address was virtually the same as that of Samuel to Saul announcing the Lord's rejection of him as king (I Sam. 15:26). In effect the prophet declared that God was already preparing to replace him and that the wheels of succession had even now begun to turn. In the so-

called messianic oracles Isaiah asserted that the Lord would
never permit his people to go leaderless or limp along under a
disobedient and faithless king. He would always provide a ruler
for them if and when they responded honestly to his covenant
grace.

It was in conjunction with the Ahaz prophecies that Isaiah
made one of his two notable contributions to the religious legacy
of the nation. Almost with the suddenness that marked the appearances of Elijah, Isaiah confronted the king who was in-
specting the defenses and water system of Jerusalem in preparation for an imminent siege by the leaders of the Syria-Israel
alliance. His message was brief, precise, but far from cryptic:

> It will not come to pass!
> For the head of Aram is Damascus
> And the head of Damascus is Rezin;
> And the head of Ephraim is Samaria,
> And the head of Samaria is the son of Remaliah.
> (7:7b–8a, 9a)

With that realistic evaluation of the haunting political peril, the
prophet made the most searching observation ever voiced—it is
really untranslatable—

> If you do not believe,
> You cannot survive.

Or as Sir George Adam Smith rendered it: "If ye have not faith,
ye cannot have staith."* That principle was repeated, near the
end of the prophet's life, when another king, Hezekiah, was
imperiled by Sennacherib (30:15–16).

---

* *The Book of Isaiah,* I (rev. ed.; New York [1928]), p. 104.

Holy, Holy, Holy

The other outstanding contribution of Isaiah was his emphasis on holiness, the Hebrew root for which occurs about thirty times in his book, though the idea pervades his whole message. It received its motivation from the call which probably came to him in the course of a temple service. It was "in the year that king Uzziah died" (ca. 742 B.C.). He must have been contemplating the life of the king, for the most part successful and commendable (II Kings 15:3; II Chron. 26:1–15) but tragically marred near its end by a spirit of pride that led him to overstep the bounds of propriety (II Chron. 26:16–21). His last years were spent in isolation from family and people because he was a leper. The Chronicler thought his affliction was due to the sin of assuming prerogatives reserved for priests. As the scenes of the king's life and activity, especially his days of uncleanness, passed through his mind, Isaiah may have caught sight of the poles of the Ark protruding from the Holy of Holies as the morning sun reflected the splendor of the visible portion of the most holy place which immediately suggested to him the contrast between the sinfulness of Uzziah and the ineffable holiness of the Lord.

In any event, he was made aware of the awful majesty of the Lord. Gazing upon the inner sanctum of the Temple he lost sight of his surroundings and beheld, in vision, the cherubs of the Ark, the throne of the Eternal, which became radiant because of the occupant. He heard their solemn antiphon as they sang the Trisagion. Cognizant of the divine presence by virtue of the enveloping cloud, he became conscious of his own condition.

> Woe to me, for I am ruined!
> Inasmuch as I am a man of polluted lips,

And live among a people of polluted lips.
For I have looked upon the King, the Lord of hosts!
(6:5)

Isaiah felt keenly his involvement in the sins of the nation and, as such, thought of himself as a personal participant in all its uncleanness.

Holiness and uncleanness are essentially cultic terms, but they have also a much wider significance. God was holy not because he was Wholly Other; he was holy because his ways and thoughts were far and away above the character of the people of the time. As Isaiah perceived, they were irreconcilable with the holy people contemplated in the covenant, which was always the perspective from which the prophets judged the life qualities of the nation. They believed that the Lord's people ought to reflect essentially the same characteristics possessed by the Lord. As we noted in an earlier chapter, they must be holy because he is holy. Holiness, therefore, carries with it an ethical connotation as well as a cultic one, as has been recognized by nearly all scholars and as, indeed, the usage of the word in the ancient world attests.

So far as Isaiah is concerned, the best illustration of the content of holiness is outlined in the first chapter of his book which, as George Fohrer has shown,* is a summary of his prophecies. There he lists the evils of the nation alongside of the demands of the holy God. To restore and maintain their covenant relationship with him, the chosen people must

Stop doing evil, learn doing good,
Seek right, check the oppressor,
Help the orphan, contend for the widow.
(1:17)

* Zeitschrift für die alttestamentliche Wissenschaft, 74 (1962), 251–68.

The hitherto faithful city has become harlotrous, she who earlier was busy with justice and righteousness was now full of murderers. Zion can be redeemed only by justice and her citizens vindicated by righteousness. Justice and righteousness alone can make her holy in the sight of the holy Lord.

XVIII

O BETHLEHEM EPHRATHAH
(Micah)

> And you, O Bethlehem Ephrathah,
>   The smallest among the tribes of Judah!
> From you shall come out to me
>   One who will be a ruler in Israel,
> And his origins are from of yore,
>   From time immemorial.   (Mic. 5:2)

The title is part of the Old Testament prophecy which has become famous as a messianic passage by virtue of its quotation by the author of Matthew's Gospel (2:5–6). It is included in the Gospel Lesson for Epiphany. In many of the church lectionaries the Old Testament Lesson for Christmas Day is taken from the fifth chapter of Micah. As it stands 5:2 is probably composite, Bethlehem having been added later. The Greek Old Testament is generally thought to preserve the more original reading which is simply, "O house of Ephrathah." In that case Bethlehem would be an explanatory addition, for Ephrathah appears to have been the name of the district in which Bethlehem was located. Hence the latter points to a more definite localization within the larger area.

Scholars have differed sharply on the question of the authenticity of the whole section of the book in which our title occurs. The position taken by this writer is the more conservative one which regards the messianic verses as genuine because they fit in so well with the thought and character of Micah, though there may be some traditio-historical adaptations and applications. Furthermore, it is altogether probable, even quite likely, that Micah visualized the need for a new ruler, just as his contemporary Isaiah did.

Moresheth-gath

For a comprehension of his attitudes and message, it is imperative to know the milieu of the prophet. In no instance is that more necessary than in that of Micah. He was a farmer-prophet, coming from Moresheth-gath in the low hill country of Judah, some twenty miles southwest of Jerusalem. Like Amos, he was thoroughly cognizant of the laws of nature as he experienced their outworkings in the agricultural pursuits of his farm. What must have impressed him even more profoundly was the sight and sound of the invading armies of Assyria when they appeared to lay siege to cities so close to his village. As a youth he may have witnessed Tiglath-pileser III's humiliation of Gaza, and later he certainly was aware of the destruction of Ashdod by Sargon II in 712 B.C. Some of his prophecies may have been inspired by Sennacherib's invasion of Palestine with the siege of Lachish, just a few miles south of Moresheth-gath. From what he saw or knew by close contact with the situation, he was convinced of the seriousness of the political exigencies that demanded resolute action on the part of the governing officials at Jerusalem if the fate that befell nearby cities was to be avoided. That was the implication of the spirited and poignant dirge by which he admonished the nation. In it he portrays devastation marching relentlessly from the Philistine plain through the hills around his hometown and on to the very gates of the capital.

In Gath do not tell it,
  Do not weep bitterly;
In Beth-leaphrah,
  In dust roll yourselves.
Traverse your way,
  O inhabitant of Shaphir,
City of shame.
  Do not go forth,
O inhabitant of Zaanan.
  The mourning garb of Bethezel,
Let its occasion be removed from you.
How can hope for good,
  The inhabitant of Maroth,
When devastation descends from Yahweh
  To the gate of Jerusalem?
Hitch the horses to the chariot,
  O inhabitant of Lachish
(The beginning of sin
  Was she to the daughter of Zion)
For to you were traced
  The transgressions of Israel.
Therefore bestow parting favors
  Upon Moresheth-gath.
The houses of Achzib [will be] a trap
  For the kings of Israel.
Again will I bring the conqueror to you,
  O inhabitant of Mareshah;
Unto Adullam will come
  The glory of Israel.
Shave [your head] and clip your hair.
  For the sons of your pleasure,
Make your baldness like the eagle's,
  For they will be exiled from you.
                    (Mic. 1:10–16)

Jerusalem

With the burden of impending misfortune weighing heavily on his mind, Micah made his way to Jerusalem to announce the word he had received from the Lord. Like the other prophets of his age, he saw that the root of the sin of Jacob was in Samaria and of that of Judah in Jerusalem. And so it was, because in the capitals of the kingdoms national policy was made. Kings resided there. There was the pulse of national life, and no nation can be stronger than the character of the leadership in the center of its activity. Basically, however, that leadership was determined and motivated by the temper of its religion, for official religion and politics were virtually identical in all ancient nations.

What was eroding the moral and spiritual strength of the people of Judah and thus inviting disaster? Precisely the same practices that undermined the Northern Kingdom. The Judean authorities were blind to the lessons of history. The more affluent cliques from the capital were extending their tentacles to the countryside which could not for long survive the drain of its resources, adverse natural conditions, and the ravages of hostile armies.

> They crave farms, and seize (them),
> And houses, and take them;
> So they crush a farmer and his household,
> A citizen with his property.   (2:2)

The heavy hand of the mortgage holders and the luxuries of officialdom in the capital divested the sturdy yeomen of their hard-earned fields and homes and brought on still further national instability. So callous had the upper classes become that they were unable to discern the right and resented interference from those who undertook to warn or correct them, especially the prophets outside of the official cult.

> "Quit complaining," they complain.
> "They ought not complain about such things."
>
> (2:6)

But Micah's most telling verbal blow is reserved for prophets, priests and princes who were directly responsible for the state of affairs including the moral bankruptcy of the nation. The religious leaders tacitly assented to the fleecing of the public because they were themselves the indirect benefactors.

> Her chiefs judge for pay,
> Her priests teach for reward,
> Her prophets divine for cash,
> Claiming to trust in the Lord, saying,
> "Is not Yahweh among us?
> Evil cannot come against us." (3:11)

No wonder local magistrates abominated right at the courts of justice and distorted the truth to gain their own ends. Together they were building Zion with the lifeblood of the poor and making Jerusalem a gigantic cesspool of guilt. They should have been making Zion the temple of righteousness and Jerusalem the city called "Yahweh is there." The only salvation for Judah, therefore, would be the destruction of the hotbed of iniquity (3:12) so that the nation (the people of God) might live.

A New Beginning

For the prophet there was but one way to go—forward, by a return to the ideals of the wilderness period of the kingdom. That is why his messiah is to be a rural prince from Bethlehem Ephrathah, the locale of the family of David. The character of the Davidic kingdom was described earlier. It was based on the principle of election, the approval of the Lord, and the covenant of brotherhood. The tribes were governed with equality and justice, there was a healthy respect for what was right and good for all Israel; priests, prophets and ruler stood in the intimate Council of the Lord who was worshiped in the way of the fathers, that is, by catering to the Ark of the Covenant and living by the desert principles associated with it—a somewhat idealized conception, to be sure.

The criteria for a renewed Zion and its ruler from the house of Ephrathah would be far less cultic and ritualistic than now. Burnt offerings, vicarious sacrifices, peace offerings would have no place in the new order. It will be again, as it was in days of old (Amos 5:25), when the sacrifices pleasing to the Lord were justice, burnt offerings loyalty to him, and peace offerings a humble walk together in covenant love before the Lord (cf. 6:6-8).

XIX

A NEW COVENANT

(Jeremiah)

Perhaps no prophecy, except those about the messiah, is more renowned than Jeremiah's proclamation of a new covenant. It has been kept alive and promulgated by the Master's declaration on the night in which he was betrayed when he took the cup, saying, "This is my blood of the (new) covenant." There may be different interpretations of what he meant, but about the source of his words there can hardly be a doubt.

Jeremiah is the one prophet about whose life experiences we know a great deal. That knowledge we owe to his own meditations and to the biographical sections of his book penned by his faithful scribe, Baruch. The most striking fact about Jeremiah is that he was a very lonely soul in the midst of a vast sea of opposition and misunderstanding. Both his political and religious adversaries failed to comprehend the importance and validity of the message he so consistently presented to them and to the people. That may have been because it is next to impossible to plumb the depths of another's experience, especially if the other person happens to be a man like Jeremiah. He was a descendant of the Abiathar family which had been exiled to Anathoth in the wake of the power struggle between Solomon and Adonijah (I Kings 2:26). (Anathoth was about two hours' walk northeast of Jerusalem.) That relationship could account, at least in part, for the suspicion that greeted the prophet on his visits to the holy city.

He was an extraordinary countryman, a man of means and standing in his own community, and a man of some leisure. He was given to study and introspective thought, as his prophecies show. He knew the history of his people, their apparent inability to maintain their side of the divine covenant. He understood the machinations of prophets, priests, and wise men. He was exceedingly well-informed on domestic and international politics. The period of his prophetic career covered the reign of five kings, two of which were of only a few months duration, and the governorship of Gedaliah (i.e., from ca. 626 to 585 B.C.).

Antecedents to the Prophecy

The New Covenant prophecy must come close to the end of Jeremiah's activity, when he despaired of the nation's survival, but before the Fall of Jerusalem. For most of his life he must have thought about the Lord's covenant, what it was, what it meant to the nation, and what it should have done for it. He was, in all probability, involved in the Josianic Reformation (II Kings 22:1–23:27) which he may have supported actively at first.

The lawbook found by Hilkiah in the Temple, in the course of preparation for repairs thereto, created consternation in the minds of king and priests. As interpreted by Huldah, the prophetess (II Kings 22:15–20), the unredressed evils of the time would lead to national disaster. The result was a speedy summons to officials and residents of Jerusalem to attend a convocation at the Temple to hear what the lawbook had to say and then decide what could be done about its directions. It was resolved to cleanse the Temple of its pagan accretions, depose the idolatrous priests in Jerusalem and the country sanctuaries outside the capital, and do away with the local high places throughout the land. The celebration of a national Passover was decreed. To casual observers the cultic renaissance had all the appearances of a great national revival of religion.

As time went on, however, Jeremiah was to discover that the resolutions of an external reformation were one thing, the sustained application of its principles to the hard and often bitter facts of life was quite another. Experience demonstrated that the Reformation produced the opposite effects of what was intended. The massive rededication to the Torah of the Lord failed to reach the lifesprings of the people. In place of humility, covenant love, and justice, pride and presumption raised their ugly heads. Josiah, the king, assumed a role far beyond that warranted by the political situation, obviously in the firm belief that now the Lord would support him in all *his* undertakings. Had he not cleansed the Temple, reinstituted the Passover, and provided for the daily sacrifices? Surely, now, he and Judah were in the good grace of God and all their exploits were his. The bubble burst when the bold king lost his life at Megiddo (II Kings 23:29; II Chron. 35:20–24). The religious authorities displayed the same spirit of arrogance, as may be gathered from references in Jeremiah's temple sermon (chs. 7, 26).

The word that came to Jeremiah from Yahweh was as follows:

Stand in the gateway of the house of Yahweh and proclaim this word there. Say, "Listen to the word of Yahweh, all (you of) Judah who enter these gates to worship Yahweh. Thus said Yahweh of hosts, God of Israel: Improve your ways and actions so that I may indeed dwell with you in this place. Place no confidence in deceptive clichés such as 'This is the Temple of

Yahweh, the Temple of Yahweh, the Temple of Yahweh!' Only if you improve your ways and actions and really deal honestly with each other, not oppressing the stranger, the orphan and the widow, or shedding innocent blood in this place, or running after other gods to your own ruin, can I dwell with you in this place, in the land that I gave to your fathers as a permanent possession. But as it is you are putting your confidence in deceptive clichés that are a mere farce. How can you steal, murder, commit adultery, swear to lies, burn incense to Baal, run after other gods of whom you are ignorant, and then come and stand before me in this house which bears my name and declare, 'We are saved'—just so you can keep on committing all these vices. Has this house which bears my name become a haven for thieves in your estimation? Indeed I myself have seen it— oracle of Yahweh!

"Just go to my earlier dwelling place that used to be at Shiloh and look what I did to it because of the misconduct of my people Israel. And now because you continue to do all these deeds, and though I admonished you again and again—oracle of Yahweh— you paid no attention and when I called you, you did not respond, therefore I am going to do to the house that bears my name and in which you place your confidence, and to the place I gave to you and your fathers, as I did to Shiloh. I will thrust you out of my sight just as I thrust out your brothers together with all the descendants of Ephraim."   (7:2–15)

They went so far as to assert that the nation was safe and secure so long as temple rites were conducted properly and the festivals observed meticulously. Yet despite all the outward manifestation or expression of piety, conditions went from bad to worse as a perusal of the final chapters of II Kings and II Chronicles proves.

The Prophecy and Its Significance

What could have gone wrong? Was the Lord's covenant a farce? Certainly not. Toward the end of his life, Jeremiah came to realize that the trouble was neither with the Lord nor with the covenant. It was with the people. And the problem, as he saw it, was how to make the divine-human relationship presupposed in the covenant operative. Too much padding had gotten between the covenant partners. Neither one came into direct contact with the other. As it was, that could come only by going through a maze of channels—priests, offerings and ceremonials of every description.

Meanwhile, in the inner recesses of his own consciousness, Jeremiah suddenly awoke to the fact that the people could be affected only by the same immediate contact with the Lord that he enjoyed. They could not, in their situation, get through to the Lord, but he could and would get through to them. In the same instant, the word of the Lord came to him: "I will make with the house of Israel and the house of Judah a new covenant" (31:31). The essential features of that new covenant were, in the words of the prophet:

1 I (Yahweh) will make a new covenant,
2 With the house of Israel and the house of Judah;
3 I will be their God and they shall be my people (cf. 7:23);
4 I will put my *torah* (= teaching) within them, that is, inscribe it on their hearts;
5 All of them will know me, from the youngest to the oldest of them;
6 I will pardon their aberrations and forget their sin.

In a nutshell, the Lord declared here his purpose to inform every person of Judah exactly as he had informed the prophet.

Jeremiah's experience taught him that few, if any, had come to know the Lord as he had. God had called him from his mother's womb, had acted upon him directly rather than through the paraphernalia of sacrifice or priesthood. Just how, he could explain only in the terms available to him. The Lord, as the scribe par excellence, had written his *torah,* his word upon his heart. That is what he would do for every Israelite "in the coming days." Jeremiah, in his own way, expressed an idea similar to that attributed to Jesus in John 3:7b—"You must be born again (anew, from above)." The covenant had to be given again, anew, from above, inscribed upon every human heart. That was the only way the Lord could deal effectively with his chosen sons.

Christians with a clearer revelation to go by can hardly miss the significance of the elemental pronouncement of Jeremiah. The new relationship with God, really not so new because he did deal with the fathers in a very personal way, rested on the individual's knowledge of the Lord. Knowledge, in the Hebrew sense, does not mean intellectual perception; it means, rather, intimate personal acquaintance, as between husband and wife, between friend and friend, the way the Master dealt with people (cf. John 15:14, 15). The concept of the divine gift of that kind of knowledge inscribed upon the heart is expressed in another way in John 6:44.

The new covenantal relationship was based upon the divine act of forgiveness of past deviations and the complete freedom from their impediments. Here one senses the impact of the older idea of nationalism. Past iniquities of the nation would be wiped out, not held against the proponents of the Lord. They would be provided with a new beginning, not as a nation but as individuals who would then become the redeemed of the Lord, the holy people.

A NEW COMMUNITY
(Ezekiel 40–48)

The Exile

The exile of Judah was due to a series of events in the area of international intrigue in which its kings became involved. After the tragic death of King Josiah at Megiddo, Jehoiakim (609–598 B.C.) was placed on the throne of the little kingdom by Pharaoh Necho of Egypt (II Kings 23:34) to whom he remained loyal throughout his reign. Because of the colossus of Mesopotamia (Nebuchadnezzar II) who began to make his power felt in the west around 601 B.C., Jehoiakim was compelled to change allegiance.

Little is known specifically of the king's maneuvers following his submission to the Babylonian monarch. That Jehoiakim was insincere is shown by the fact that he withheld tribute in 598 B.C., that is, he rebelled. That quickly brought Nebuchadnezzar to the west, but Jehoiakim died before the siege of the capital began. His eighteen-year-old son was no match for the seasoned Babylonian king and so capitulated. Jehoiachin and the cream of the country were taken to Babylon, and Zedekiah, his uncle, was placed on the throne as a vassal of Babylon.

He was a weak ruler; most of the power appears to have been wielded by the court officials. His intentions were doubtless good, judged by the fact that he frequently sided with Jeremiah against the latter's persecutors. On occasion the king called upon the prophet for advice. Flirting with Egypt continued at every opportunity. Finally, at the instigation of Egyptian agents, a full-scale revolt, in the form of refusal to remit tribute, broke out against Babylon about 589 B.C.

That was the beginning of the end. Jerusalem fell in 587 B.C.; King Zedekiah had his eyes put out and then was doomed to languish in a Babylonian prison the rest of his life. The High Priest Seraiah, his assistant, and the leaders and officials of the court were dispatched by Nebuchadnezzar at Riblah.

Jeremiah, Habakkuk and Ezekiel were deeply involved in the struggle that led to the downfall of Judah and its exile. Jeremiah, in particular, had the mind and viewpoint of a statesman. For him the critical events of the age were due to the intervention of the Lord whose mighty hand was evident in the outworking of history. Judah was his people who had been summoned to his service. As such they were pledged to reflect his character and will in their own country, but also elsewhere in the world.

Jeremiah recognized in the king of Babylon not only the instrument for the punishment of Judah for its immoralities, injustices, oppressions, and defection from the Lord, but also that of promoting his plan for the world (cf. Jer. 27:6 where he is referred to as "my servant"). Denationalization would really forward the Lord's design, bursting the bonds that were hampering it and freeing his people to become missionaries to the world. Babylon was the Lord's instrument, as Assyria had been earlier (Is. 10:5–12), to uproot those things in which the nation was placing a false confidence, and offered an opportunity for the transplantation of his people in a scheme of service to mankind. Jeremiah advised the exiles to accept the discipline of the Lord, work in the vineyard of Babylon and, in due time, they would again be restored to their land with, perhaps, a broader vision of the purpose for their existence.

Ezekiel

Ezekiel is the least read of the major prophets, possibly because of the cryptic visions that make his message hard to understand without a thorough knowledge of ancient history and mythology. His strange actions and the peculiarities associated with his various experiences have led some to regard him as a psychopath. That his behavior was strange requires no other proof than the reading of his book. But to charge him with mental imbalance is quite another matter. He was a sensitive man, subjected to historical circumstances enough to produce abnormal reactions from the most psychologically stable of men.

According to the superscription of his book, Ezekiel was one of those deported to Babylon by Nebuchadnezzar II in the first captivity (15/16 March 597 B.C.). So he must have belonged to the better classes of citizens (II Kings 24:14–16); he was the scion of a priestly family. That accounts for his strong accent on cultic purity present in his prophecies. It would appear that most, if not quite all of his prophetic ministry was carried out in exile. Its importance can hardly be over-exaggerated because, as subsequent events were to prove, it was in Babylon among the cultured golah (exiles) that the religious community was preserved. Only the poor, less stable elements of the Judean population were left in the land. Two later deportations virtually excluded the possibility of any significant residue of Yahwism left in the homeland to maintain a vital and orthodox religious organization.

In Babylon

The deportees were settled on the Chebar Canal, somewhere in the vicinity of Nippur. To judge from our prophet, the letter of Jeremiah (29:4–23), and archaeological discoveries, they fared extremely well in their new home. That they were religiously depressed at first (Ps. 137) is to be expected, but that condition was temporary. The Babylonian Jewish community may have been assisted in regaining its composure and in developing a new perspective of hope for restoration by virtue of the fact that Jehoiachin was still alive and hence the legitimate king. Had he and his family suffered the fate that overtook Zedekiah, things could have been very different.

Jehozadak, the son of Seraiah (I Chron. 6:14) who was executed by Nebuchadnezzar at Riblah (II Kings 25:18–21; Jer. 52:24–27), was High Priest but nowhere is he spoken of as an active participant in the religious affairs of the exilic community. During the early days of the exile Ezekiel seems to have occupied a crucial position. His home was the assembly center (8:1; 14:1; 20:1) where the darkening embers of religion were fanned. The exiles were addressed almost regularly as "the house of Israel," a fact that may have had much to do with the development of the religious climate reflected later by the Chronicler and, indeed, in creating the temper for the post-exilic religious establishment in Judah.

Around the prophet, in his own house, gathered officials and elders to hear the word of the Lord and for mutual encouragement in the faith. On certain occasions Ezekiel was inspired to utter oracles dealing with faraway events (cf. chs. 8, 14). Chapter 20 records an oracle delivered to the elders at their request—"they came to consult Yahweh." There was neither altar nor ceremony; in fact there was no place for either. The prophet's dwelling place became the locale for devotion and hearing the word of the Lord. Many scholars think the Synagogue originated in the Ezekielian fellowship in exile as an organization for study, prayer and exhortation. Some of the observations recorded in the book of the prophet certainly lend themselves to that supposition. In a word, Ezekiel developed the functions of the pastor.

Vision of a New Community

If what has just been written is true, then, we take it, Ezekiel's prime motive for instructing his compatriots was not merely to hold them together, it was rather to initiate a kind of holy society in preparation for more auspicious things on the day when the Lord would restore Israel. He spoke often of restoration, but the most outstanding vision on this score was that depicting a valley of dry bones (37:1–14) suddenly taking on flesh and sinews and animated by the divine Spirit. The vision may have been inspired by the sight of a battlefield strewn with the bones of slain corpses which subsequently, in the vividness of the prophet's imagination, reminded him of defeated and decadent Israel. His profound faith in the restorative will and power of God then conjured up for him the mental picture of a revived, resurrected people.

Reassured by that vision—that God will return his people to their homeland—he was soon to have another. This time he was led in spirit "to the land of Israel" (40:2) where the Lord showed him a whole new community whose nucleus was "a building laid out like a city." That was the New Temple whose structure, position, arrangements and furnishings duplicate those of the Solomonic edifice, but with emphasis on magnitude and perfection. It had two courts, an outer and an inner, whose purpose was to keep separate the clean and the unclean—again an accentuation upon the holy dwelling place of the holy God surrounded by a holy people. To this holy place the glory of the Lord is visualized as returning (43:1-9) in the same manner in which it was seen to withdraw (ch. 10) before unholy hands had laid in ashes the old city and Temple.

After the glory of the Lord had taken up its abode in the New Temple, the prophet's attention was directed to the cultus with its consecrated altar (43:10-27), its sanctified and strictly regulated priesthood (44:1-45:17), and the worship of regular and festival offerings (45:18-46:15). The new structure is the source of (the water of) life (47:1-12) flowing through the land and fructifying it. Once more the whole land will be parceled out to the twelve tribes as it was in the days of Joshua. Over the land will rule a prince who will have a special portion within which will be the allotment of the Levites and the city itself. The holy city will henceforth be known as "Yahweh-shammah" (= Yahweh is there).

In some respects Ezekiel's new community represents a regression from the prophetic ideal. It surely lacks the world-wide vision of the Second Isaiah (49:6). Yet the community is a redeemed one, holy to the Lord. That is why no alien may set foot in it. No prophet is there because the Lord God himself is in the midst of it. In a sense it is a colony of heaven. But the prophet's conception of exclusiveness must not be judged too adversely. After all, he resided in a pagan environment and the old land was defiled—that is why it was in a state of desolation. The chief contribution of this exilic prophet was his insistence upon the preservation of the remnant of the holy people, the seed of the Lord, from submergence by the pagan society of Babylon. The times and situation demanded the strengthening of the things that remained so that in due course its saving influence could be extended. Ezekiel's vision of a new community became the pattern for another great vision—that of the New Jerusalem (Rev. 21).

XXI

PROPHETS AND PROPHETS
(Zephaniah, Nahum, Habakkuk)

Sometimes the Minor Prophets are shortchanged by Bible students and expositors, though upon closer examination they often turn out to be of tremendous significance, not only for an understanding of religio-historical developments in Israel, but more importantly for a better comprehension of the theology of the Old Testament. Their words would hardly have been remembered or included in the canon of Scripture if they had not impressed profoundly their contemporaries and the later Jewish theologians.

They throw welcome light on more than one occasion or situation otherwise totally obscure. That is true of the three prophets to which attention is directed in this chapter. Each of them has not only a message of his own but helps us gauge the temper of Judah in the age in which they lived. All three were active during the last thirty years of the seventh century. So far as we can determine, they did not measurably influence the course of history directly, but they did, nevertheless, profoundly affect the total pattern of thought wrought out in those hectic years.

Zephaniah
Zephaniah's period is disputed. He has been placed both before the Deuteronomic Reformation and after its magnificent failure.

Good arguments have been presented for each date, but the writer believes the message of Zephaniah fits best into the situation around 630 B.C., or just about a decade before the noble experiment of 621 B.C. (See chapter XIX.)

His prophecy could not have been very encouraging to the people of Judah since it has to do almost exclusively with the Day of the Lord which, for Zephaniah, is one of doom and utter destruction. The first words of his first sermon must have sent a chill down the spine of the audience.

> I will make a clean sweep of everything,
> From the face of the ground,
> I will make a clean sweep of man and beast;
> . . . .
> I will cut off man from upon the face of the ground.
>
> (1:2, 3)

Then, like Amos (5:1-2), he proceeded to sing a bitter dirge on the character of the Day (1:14-18), which inspired Thomas of Celano's hymn, Dies Irae (= Day of Wrath). Yet, perhaps, Zephaniah's Day of the Lord is to be viewed rather as a day for the consuming of the nation's dross than as one of indiscriminate extermination (cf. 3:8-13).

The violent outburst of the prophet can be understood best in the light of what transpired in Judah in the decade before 630 B.C. Josiah had occupied the throne for about ten years, supported by people and leaders. But nothing concrete had been accomplished in removing the moral and religious filth that had accumulated in the reigns of Manasseh (687-642 B.C.) and Amon (642-640 B.C.). Though the king was very young, his advisers could have encouraged him to take steps toward that end. But they did not. Time was growing short, for the instability of world politics—Judah was doubtless still a vassal of Assyria—

required the utmost urgency. A few years later the wheels of world convulsion were to begin to turn, bringing a new master in the person of Nabopolassar, the Chaldaean.

Zephaniah may not have had much of a constructive nature to offer, but he did succeed in awakening a concern for the Lord. For shortly afterward another, greater voice was heard in the land—that of Jeremiah. If our prophet preached at the time indicated above, Jeremiah could certainly have been aroused to activity by his stern admonitions.

Nahum

Nahum belongs some time around 612 B.C., the year the colossus on the Tigris, Nineveh, fell. He is more of a singer than a prophet; his message consists largely of songs celebrating that event. His first poem announces the inevitable judgment of the Lord upon evil. The Lord is a zealous God, one who vindicates the righteous. He is long-suffering, even to his enemies, but there comes a time when he will act (1:3). Nahum exhibits a fine sense of justice and discernment in pointing out that

> The Lord is good to those that wait for him,
> A fortress in the day of distress.
> He knows those whose refuge is in him.
>
> (1:7)

Nineveh, whose cruelties and oppressions had tormented the world, will be brought down with a crash. Those who respect and trust in the Lord will be spared. Evildoers cannot forever succeed or the righteous forever suffer humiliation and defeat. In one of the most powerful poems in the Bible, Nahum describes the siege and fall of the Assyrian capital (2:1–12; 3:1–19).

The cadence of the original Hebrew enables the reader to hear the galloping chariots, the clash of armor, the screaming

victims, and the waters rushing through river channels opened
to flood the city. No amount of preparation (3:14–15) can stave
off the destined event. The iniquity of the city is so overwhelming that nothing can halt her plunge over the precipice of disaster. Great as Nineveh was in the world of her time, in the vast
expanse of God's realm her princes were like grasshoppers in
his sight; her vaunted merchant colonies evaporated like fleeing
locusts; her officials and clerks as parasitic and fleeting as be-
numbed grasshoppers reanimated by the warming sun (3:16–
17). The relentless judgment of the universe has at last caught
up with the proud and haughty nation.

Habakkuk

There is no sufficient clear-cut evidence to date Habakkuk exactly. Broadly speaking, he falls some time in the Chaldaean
period, most probably near the end of the seventh century. His
prophecy may have arisen from threats to Judah involved in
the last battle between the army of Nebuchadnezzar II and the
Egyptian-Assyrian allies fought at Carchemish on the Euphrates
in 605 B.C. He may have had the coming storm in mind in 1:5–6,
or else was moved by it to issue a warning to Judah to beware of
its consequences for her. Judah was still a vassal of Egypt, which
position was imposed upon her by virtue of the defeat of Josiah
at Megiddo in 609 B.C. Pharaoh Necho II had put Eliakim
(Jehoiakim) on the throne, and he remained a puppet of the
Egyptian monarch. The years following the rout of the allies at
Carchemish were fraught with peril for the little country caught
in the coils of world politics.

Jehoiakim was under heavy tribute to Egypt (II Kings 23:35)
that required the exaction of taxes beyond the capability of many
to pay. It is not impossible that the more affluent and unscrupu-

lous citizens attempted to evade their share of the levy by shifting the burden to the poorer and defenseless classes. Such injustices may underlie the declaration

> The *torah* is benumbed,
> And judgment is never exercised,
> For the wicked outmaneuver the righteous;
> Hence fallacious judgment is exercised.
>
> (1:4)

The celebrated passage of Habakkuk 2:4 (quoted in Rom. 1:17; Gal. 3:11; Heb. 10:38) grew out of a singular boldness on the part of the prophet. Observing the rapid movement of the neo-Babylonians, sweeping away everything in their path, he puts to the Lord one of the most vexing questions man can ask. Habakkuk was not ignorant of the wickedness of Judah and did not attempt to dispute the judgment about to overtake her, but neither could he understand why "the wicked swallows up the man who is more righteous than himself" (1:13). That was the query he posed to the Lord. Then, taking up his position on the watchtower of devotion, he waited for a reply. It was not long in coming. The Lord made no distinction in degree of wickedness. Hebrews and Babylonians alike were guilty before him. Therefore neither would escape with impunity.

> Verily, he who is not upright is vulnerable,
> But the righteous man shall live by his faithfulness.
> Though he be crafty as Hiyon,
> A faithless man will not succeed.   (2:4–5)

SPEAKING TO THE HEART OF JERUSALEM
(Isaiah 40–66)

Isaiah 40–66 represents the high water mark of Old Testament prophecy. The author has been called the "evangelist" of the Old Testament. The relative importance of his work for the writers of the New Testament may be judged from the fact that passages from it are quoted or referred to in sixteen of its twenty-seven books and that these quotations come from twenty-six of the twenty-seven chapters of this section of Isaiah. Ninety-six verses are quoted or alluded to in one hundred and ten verses of the New Testament. Three verses of Isaiah 40–66 are quoted four times, three three times, and twenty-one two times.

Most scholars regard this portion of our present book of Isaiah as the contribution of another author or authors than Isaiah of Jerusalem. That chapters 40–66 do not come from the period of ca. 740–700 B.C. may be seen from historical and personal references, the language, metric structure and vocabulary. Then, too, there is the tone of these oracles that lack the virulent feature of judgment and denunciation appearing in chapters 1–39. This portion of Isaiah exhibits an atmosphere of deliverance and joy, a people chastened and forgiven.

Deliverance

Isaiah 40:1–11 sets the theme for the major portion of the prophetic discourses.

> Cheer up, cheer up, my people,
>   Says your God.
> Speak to the heart of Jerusalem;
>   Announce to her
> That her campaign is over,
>   That her iniquity is forgiven,
> That she has received from Yahweh's hand,
>   Double [punishment] for all her sins.
>
> A voice cries:
> "In the wilderness clear
>   The way of Yahweh,
> Level in the steppe
>   A highway for our God.
> Let every valley be raised up,
>   Every mountain and hill lowered,
> The crooked paths become straight,
>   The rugged places a broad valley.
> Then the glory of Yahweh will appear
>   And all flesh shall see it together,
> For the mouth of Yahweh has said it."
>
> A voice cries, "Announce."
>   But I said, "What shall I announce?"
> —"All flesh is grass,
>   And all its strength like the flower of the field;
> The grass dries up,
>   The flower fades,
>   When the wind of Yahweh
>   Blows over it.
> (Verily, the people is [like] grass.)

The grass dries up,
The flower fades,
But the word of our God
Stands forever."
Upon a high mountain climb,
O evangelist of Zion,
Raise with vigor your voice,
O evangelist of Jerusalem,
Raise [it] fearlessly,
Tell the cities of Judah,
"Here is your God!"
Here is Yahweh God,
He comes with power,
His arm controls it;
Look, his reward is with him,
And his wages before him.
Like a shepherd he cares for his flock,
With his arms he gathers the lambs,
And carries [them] in his bosom;
He gently leads those giving suck.

As in the prologue of the book of Job, the scene of the first proclamation is set in the heavens. The prophet listened to the con-
versation between the members of the Heavenly Council to
which he had been admitted (cf. Amos 3:7). There he heard
the Lord summoning his messengers to the task he had laid out
for them.

The charges of the Lord, like prophetic oracles generally, are
short and to the point. The first directive is a general one, speaking of comfort for the suffering and enslaved people. This is followed by a series of heavenly choral responses, each emphasizing
the certainty and eternity of the word of the Lord. Then Zion
and Jerusalem are addressed and, having already been made
aware of the good news, are exhorted to pass it on to the cities

of Judah. Read with the following sequence in mind, the cumulative force of the decisions of the Council of the Lord is striking.

1   The address of the Lord (vss. 1-2)
2   Response of the first messenger (vss. 3-5)
3   Response of the second messenger (vss. 6-8)
4   Response of the third messenger (vs. 9)
5   Announcement of the fourth messenger (vss. 10-11)

The prophet heard Yahweh call for the comforting of his people. No more threats, no further reference to sin and guilt, except to affirm pardon for them. To comfort meant to strengthen, support, uphold, console this people which had endured so much by virtue of the false perspectives held before it earlier by a deluded, recalcitrant, power-crazy, materialistically minded court and cult. For nearly half a century it had languished in exile, its more perceptive adherents improvising all sorts of ways to keep faith alive, its prophets and teachers active attempting to maintain what often seemed to be deceptive hope. It was difficult for the people to travel once more the way of the wilderness of Babylon until all the aberrant generation had passed away. Now the time had come for deliverance, for the crossing of another Reed Sea, another Jordan—this time the desert journey and reconstruction that would not be pushed aside miraculously by the divine hand but which would have to be carried out by their own efforts. But more about this in the next chapter.

Suffice it to say here that a new star had risen in the east. The hosts of Cyrus II of Anshan, since about 547 B.C., swept back and forth between Asia Minor and Persia and now threatened Nabonidus, the last of the Babylonian kings. All manner of wild rumors flooded the city of Babylon and must have raised the hopes of its captive peoples, but none more so than those of the

Jews whose chief joy always was Jerusalem (Ps. 137:6). That was the historical atmosphere in which the prophet heard the welcome word of comfort from the head of the Heavenly Council.

It was a time for wooing, not condemnation. Now had arrived the day of which Hosea dreamed—the Lord speaking to the heart of Jerusalem. That was the language and way of love. And it heralded a new beginning, for old things were done with. The period of debt service had been paid in full, the account of the nation's deviations settled. The idea of double payment may be due to the fact that more than forty years, the round number of years spent in the wilderness, had elapsed since the beginning of the captivity in 587 B.C.

Next the first and second messengers of the Council sang of the word of the Lord—the word of deliverance which was about to become evident to "all flesh together," that word that "stands forever." God's word and his promises are eternal. Everything else is transient. The third and fourth messengers announced the good news to Jerusalem and Zion, which are personalized, and then exhorted to spread the "gospel" (the Greek actually uses the word evangelist), telling of the salvation of the Lord reflected in his shepherding activity (vs. 11).

The Servant

Our prophet was privileged to go beyond his predecessors because of his experiences and what he heard and saw in the higher councils of faith. He peered far beyond the present salvation to the strange but effective way of Yahweh. That was the way of service and endurance. The awful price of sin was always suffering, exile, death. Yet it was somehow through them that a new lease on life was given.

From the earliest days God's servants suffered—far beyond their personal deserts when compared with others who often went scot-free. That was true especially of such men as Moses, Elijah and Jeremiah. But in the exilic experience Israel itself, God's son, had been subjected to a crucial agony wholly out of proportion to what others received for their deeds. That was the problem that concerned Habakkuk. Now the revelation of the Lord became clearer in the vision of the Second Isaiah.

In four classic poems he puts before the world what he had seen and heard. The first (42:1-4) sets forth the work of the Lord's servant who, in all probability here is Israel corporately conceived, as so often in the Psalms. The Servant's role was "to bring judgment to the nations" (vs. 1), that is, to illustrate the way of right and the meaning of the *torah* (= teaching) of the Lord (vs. 4).

> Behold, my servant whom I support,
>   My chosen one in whom I delight;
> I have put my spirit upon him,
>   My judgment he will execute among the nations.
> He will neither shout nor make himself conspicuous,
>   And he will not make his voice resound in the street.
> A crushed reed he will not shatter,
>   And a dimming wick he will not put out.
> Faithfully will he execute judgment.
>   He will not desist or be discouraged,
> Until he establish judgment in the earth,
>   And the distant shores wait hopefully for his instruction.
>   (42:1-4)

That would not be easy as may be seen from the other three poems. The Servant's lot (49:1-6) often seems futile (vs. 4), but by the grace and power of the Lord he will serve as "a light

of the nations, to extend my salvation to the ends of the earth"
(vs. 6).

> Listen to me, O distant shores,
>> And take note, O peoples from afar!
> Yahweh has called me from the belly,
>> From the womb of my mother he has chosen me;
> He made my mouth like a keen-edged sword,
>> By the shadow of his hand he concealed me;
> He made me like a finished arrow,
>> In his quiver he kept me hidden.
> He said to me, "My servant are you,
>> O Israel, in whom I will glorify myself."
> But I said, "In vain have I striven,
>> Fruitlessly and for nought have I exhausted my strength;
> Yet assuredly my justification is with Yahweh,
>> And my compensation with my God."
> And now, said Yahweh
>> Who molded me from the belly to be his servant,
> To bring back Jacob unto him,
>> That Israel be gathered together to him,
> When I am respected in the sight of Yahweh,
>> And my God is my strength:
> "It is not enough for you to be (simply) my servant
>> To re-establish the tribes of Jacob,
> And to rehabilitate those of Israel who have been preserved;
>> I am also appointing you to be a light for the nations,
> To be my salvation
>> To the ends of the earth.   (49:1–6)

Yet he is under the discipline of the Lord (50:4–9) and, despite
humiliation (vs. 6), will not rest until he has completed his
mission.

> The Lord Yahweh has given me
>> The tongue of the learned,

To know how to encourage the weary with speech.
  He awakens (me) morning by morning,
    He awakens my ear
      To listen as learners do.
The Lord Yahweh has opened my ear,
  And I have not been stubborn,
    Nor did I retreat.
My back I offered to the smiters,
  My cheeks to those who pull out the hair.
My face I turned not away
  From dishonor and spittle.
Because the Lord Yahweh (always) helps me,
  I have not been disconcerted;
Therefore I have set
  My face like diamond,
    For I know I shall never be dishonored.
My vindicator is at hand;
  Who will argue with me?
    Let us stand up together (for judgment).
Who is my opponent?
  Let him approach me.
Behold, the Lord Yahweh helps me;
  Who is the one to declare me guilty?
Behold, all of them wear out like clothes,
  A moth consumes them.   (50:4-9)

From all this it is clear that God's victory in the world comes about only through suffering (52:13–53:12). And it is a vicarious suffering. When the blinded eyes of the nations are opened to the truth they will see and understand that it was their sicknesses he bore, their pains he endured, that he was pierced by their rebellions, crushed by their iniquities (vs. 4).

Behold, my servant is pious,
  He is lifted up
    And very highly exalted.

As many were astounded by him,
  For his appearance was so different from (other) men,
    And his bearing from that of the sons of man.
For he startles many nations;
  Concerning him kings are speechless;
For what was not explained to them they saw,
  And what they had not understood they (now) discerned.
Who could have believed our report,
  And the arm of Yahweh, concerning whom was it disclosed?
Like a suckling (child) he grew up in our presence,
  Like a shoot out of the arid ground;
There was no comeliness about him or majesty,
    That we should have taken note of him, nor imposing appearance,
      That we might admire him.
He was ignored and abandoned by men,
  One of pains and acquainted with sickness;
And as one hiding (his) face from us
  He was ignored and we did not notice him.
Verily it was he who bore our sickness,
  And he endured our pains,
While we reckoned him plagued,
  Smitten of God and afflicted.
Moreover, he was pierced by our rebellions,
  Crushed on account of our iniquities;
The chastisement of our peace was upon him,
  And by his wounds healing came to us.
All of us, like sheep, have wandered about (aimlessly),
  We turned each one to his own way,
While Yahweh smote him
  For the waywardness of us all.
He was mishandled and oppressed,
  But never opened his mouth;
Just as a sheep is brought to the slaughter,
  And as a ewe before her shearers,
    He was silent and never opened his mouth.
From protective judgment he was snatched,

And among his generation, who gave (it) thought?
He was cut off from the land of the living:
  For the rebellion of his people was he smitten.
His grave was made with the wicked,
  And with the rich in his death;
Although he was not guilty of violence,
  And there was no deception in his mouth.
Yet Yahweh willed to crush him grievously—
  If he offers a guilt offering
    He shall see descendants,
  He shall prolong (his) days,
  And Yahweh's will
    Shall prosper in his hand.
From his travail he comprehends,
  The righteous one is content when he understands;
My servant justifies many
  And bears their iniquities.
Therefore I will allot him a portion among the great,
  And with the powerful will he divide booty
Because he devoted himself utterly (even to death),
  And was numbered with transgressors,
And bore the sin of many,
  And was smitten for transgressors.   (52:13–53:12)

Imperfect servant that Israel was, she was God's light and salvation to the nations. Israel was the matrix of Jesus Christ who took upon himself the form of a servant, patterned his life after Isaiah's servant and then exhorted his followers to do the same.

XXIII

PROPHETS OF A NEW ISRAEL
(Haggai and Zechariah)

How significant it is that God raised up men with bold ideas for each situation in the life and history of his people. When they needed chastisement his prophets were ready to wield the rod of word and act, when direction was indicated holy men were invested with the way of the *torah* (= teaching), when comfort and strengthening were called for evangelists were moved to utter words of encouragement and to offer plans for the revival of the remnant. God has always provided for his people in the most varied circumstances of their experience.

When the Second Isaiah delivered his stirring, heart-warming message, new hope sprang forth in the hearts and souls of the Babylonian exiles. That hope was accentuated by the decree of Cyrus permitting those Jews who were minded to do so to return to Jerusalem and Judah with a view toward the re-establishment of their sacred institutions (Ezra 1:1–4). The rescript of the Persian king was not just permissive; it offered definite, tangible incentives for the Jews to return, possibly as much political in motive as religious. It would be advantageous to have a friendly community on the outskirts of his empire, on the frontier of Egypt which was destined to produce complications for him a little later.

The Changed Situation

Just how many of the exiles actually returned to the homeland is difficult to determine at present because the figures given in Ezra (2:64 ff.) are based on later summaries which do not reflect the situation of 538 B.C. But that a goodly number did respond to the royal invitation is certain. The Jewish officials involved in carrying out the edict of Cyrus were Sheshbazzar, a scion of the royal family of Judah—actually a son of Jehoiachin—and Joshua, the High Priest. Progress in the momentous task of building the new community is hard to assess, though it could not have been phenomenal as may be seen from conditions of land and people depicted in the two prophecies outlined below. Rehabilitation required more than a royal decree or even than material support for the religious enterprises to be undertaken.

The very first contingent of repatriates (the *golah*) apparently met with serious opposition from the Samaritans who had gradually taken over the territory around Jerusalem after the fiasco under Gedaliah in 585 B.C. and now claimed hegemony over it, though it had never been officially assigned to them by either the Babylonians or their Persian successors. Nor had outsiders been settled there, as was the case in Samaria after the Assyrian conquest. There was to all intents and purposes simply a power vacuum that had slowly been filled by the Samaritans and other surrounding peoples, including the poorer classes of Jews who had, in one way or another, escaped deportation.

Evidence seems to indicate that the *golah* too were poor and certainly not well organized, though they were doubtless full of religious zeal. First they rebuilt the altar (Ezra 3:2–3) so as to carry on at least a modicum of worship such as daily sacrifices and festival celebrations (Ezra 3:4–6a). Then they undertook to implement the main provision of the Cyrus decree—the rebuilding of the Temple. Timber, supplies, craftsmen and workmen were assembled for the work which is said to have begun in the second year after the return (Ezra 3:8).

The beginning consisted only of laying the foundation of the Temple. Then they hit a snag in the form of opposition, for the most part because their project appeared offensive to the people of Samaria (Ezra 4:1–3) whose request for permission to participate therein they had rejected. It was not reconstruction that occasioned offense, but the fact that the people of the land were excluded from worship because they were regarded as unclean and hence ceremonially unacceptable to the pure Jews just returned from Babylon. For them to have permitted the Samaritans and "people of the land" to participate would have meant a compromise of faith. Insistence upon exclusiveness thus produced friction which, with natural adversities, resulted in halting the work of rebuilding the Temple.

Haggai and Zechariah

This is where Haggai and Zechariah, the prophets of reconstruction, came in. They were contemporaries. Both were active in the second year of the reign of King Darius I (520 B.C.). Neither of them were at all like their pre-exilic predecessors. They had no creative message. Their objective was to strengthen the things that remained, to provide a sort of holding operation upon which the future might capitalize. Conflict with Samaria and the people of the land generated a kind of religious lethargy among the *golah* while at the same time they endeavored to strengthen their position by way of economic aggrandizement. But in so doing, they were in serious danger of losing their zeal for the very purpose they came to achieve. They had, in effect, put second things first.

Haggai reminded them of their paneled houses and observed that material blessings seemed so evanescent "because of my house which lies in ruins while you yourselves look each after his own house" (1:9). His proclamation was heeded, for Zerubbabel and Joshua were aroused and by their exhortation the people were stirred to action. So encouraged was the prophet by the popular response that he was moved to spur on the authorities by the promise of a glorious future: "The coming splendor of this house will surpass that of the past" (2:9). Along with it went the firing of a messianic hope that may have brought a swift reaction from the authorities since Zerubbabel soon disappeared from the scene.

Two months after Haggai's initial sermons came Zechariah whose message was, in many respects, like that of his contemporary (1:16–17). His series of visions exhibit a soaring faith in the Lord. He calls to witness the former prophets (1:4; 7:12) as testimony to the validity of the promises of the Lord. His conception of a world-wide appeal of the Jewish faith is expressed in the following quotations:

> In that day many nations shall associate themselves with Yahweh and shall become my people; and I will dwell among you, and you shall know that Yahweh of hosts has sent me unto you.
> (Zech. 2:11 = 2:15 in the Hebrew text)

> From far and wide they will come and rebuild the temple of Yahweh, and you shall know that Yahweh of hosts has sent me unto you. And that will happen if you really listen to the voice of Yahweh your God.   (Zech. 6:15)

> Yahweh of hosts spoke as follows: "In those days ten men from nations of every language shall grasp hold of the garment of a

Jew saying, 'Permit us to go with you, for we have heard that
God is with you.'"   (Zech. 8:23)

is echoed in the declaration of Jesus in Matthew 8:11:

> I tell you, many from east and west shall come and recline with
> Abraham, Isaac and Jacob in the kingdom of heaven.

The realization of the dicta of the prophets would come about
by the instrumentality of the Spirit of the Lord rather than
through human initiative (4:6). Something of the old prophets
comes alive in Zechariah in his demand for the love of faithfulness and peace as essential for the progress of the new community:

> The fasts of the fourth, the fifth, the seventh, and the tenth
> months will be joyous and happy occasions, delightful festivals:
> therefore love faithfulness and peace.   (Zech. 8:19)

Ceremonial alone was not enough.

Institutionalism with a Purpose

From one point of view the reader, familiar with the other prophets, especially the Second Isaiah, receives a chill from these
prophets. The creative spirit and the Yahwistic fire of the great
religious enthusiasts of the pre-exilic age are almost totally absent. But from another vantage point, Haggai and Zechariah too
were men of the hour. They saw clearly that without a religious
community incarnate in the institutions of Temple and sacrifice
and festival, the religion of the fathers would perish. Religion
may well be berated severely when it loses sight of the covenant
of love for individuals within the brotherhood of the sons of
God, but there are occasions when the individual would be lost

without the framework of that brotherhood held together by the
worshiping community. The period of Haggai and Zechariah
was one that demanded accentuation upon the latter in the birth
throes of a new Israel.

XXIV

GIFTS OF WISDOM
(Proverbs)

"How," inquires the Psalmist, "can a young man keep clean his behavior?" (119:9). That is the haunting question confronting parents and seriously minded young people today. Those concerned with maintaining the family name and character have always sought a satisfactory way not only of holding to a specific course in life but of improving it. The author of the Psalm suggests it may be done "by keeping (observing) thy word" (or words, as in the versions).

"Thy word" (or words) was the word of the Lord. But what word is meant? Where is it to be found? How does it apply specifically to one seeking direction in the ordinary conduct of life?

Questions are tantalizingly easy to raise, but only wise persons can find or supply answers. Sometimes they too are baffled, though they may work at it long and hard as did Israel's wisdom teachers. The prophets and priests dealt, for the most part, with the social unit, that is, the tribe, clan, family or nation. They gave direction in accordance with the word of the Lord as they were moved by direct inspiration or as it was given them in the intimate Council of the Lord. Not so the great wisdom teachers. True, they were inspired servants of the Lord and delivered his word, or perhaps better, applied his word to the needs of individual and community. The wise men were occupied with the task of preventing the inner moral decay of persons and families so that the national calamity threatened by the prophets could be averted.

Proverbs

What then were the Proverbs, the teachings of the wise? They were not simply pious aphorisms or high-sounding couplets or quatrains designed for entertainment. Nor were they riddles to be solved like the teaser proposed by Samson for Delilah, "From the eater came something to eat, From the strong came something sweet" (Judg. 14:14), or eudaemonistic directives intended to show young people how to enjoy life without effort. Israel's wise men were gifted personalities, endowed with a profound sensitivity for the outworking of the laws of the moral universe. As Helmut Gese said recently, they were cognizant of the order of the universe, the principles by which it operated, and their observations were grounded in that perception.*

Physical and social science teach us that there is another sphere of revelation, that of the natural and moral order, which is also from God and reflects the way of Creation, the way God works. There is an order and purpose behind the universe and life. That is what the wise men saw and why they emphasized the necessity for the acquisition of wisdom which, for them, was "the ability to assess truly the values of life." Wisdom enabled one to understand, interpret and apply to life the fundamental laws of the universe, which also were word of God wrought out in the

---

* *Lehre und Wirklichkeit in der alten Weisheit* (Tübingen, 1958), p. 33.

nature of things. The wise men possessed a knowledge of that word as it manifested itself in the order of creation. They endeavored to help others to see and observe the principles operative in the order of creation that they might attain the happiness-blessedness intended by the Creator.

The Book

The book of Proverbs, one of the major wisdom writings in the Old Testament, represents a compilation of materials developed and collected over many centuries. It bears the name of Solomon, probably on the basis of the tradition recorded in I Kings 4:29–34. While the king doubtless dabbled in that kind of wisdom, he appears to have been much more concerned about what would be referred to today as natural science—knowledge of trees, plants, animals, birds, reptiles and fish. He did, however, also possess the power of discernment in other matters. Nevertheless his life tells against the exalted moral standards reflected in our book.

There are at least eight major collections, several of them composed of smaller ones. A number of these collections contain a whole host of materials drawn from foreign sources, especially from Egypt. They probably came into Israel through Canaan. Some may have come from Southern Arabia. All of which shows how widely current in the ancient world the observations and teachings of wisdom were.

Lessons of Wisdom

The underlying principle of the instruction of the wise men of Israel was the fear of or reverence for the Lord. That phrase occurs more often in Proverbs than in any other book of the Bible. Naturally many of the outstanding doctrines of the Old Testament do not appear in Proverbs—for instance, the Sabbath, messianism, Passover, feasts, Temple, priests, prophets are not even mentioned. They belong to another order. In a sense Proverbs represents a fulfillment of the religious life, its expression in the daily round. As such it is not supplementary but complementary to the other great literature of Israel.

It is possible to call attention here to only a few of the outstanding problems of life dealt with by the writers—problems that are as alive today as in ancient Israel. Most of the observations and teachings are in the form of warnings to the youth of the nation. One of them has to do with the attitude and character of fools. No less than five kinds of fools are mentioned. One is the young fool, a youth without experience but still teachable. Another is possessed of obstinate stupidity, one who delights in wrongdoing and is proud of it. A third adds licentiousness to obstinate stupidity. This kind of fool has a mind of his own; he refuses correction. Then there is the scorner who is an enemy of God, man and himself. He is arrogant, quarrelsome, mischievous and sets the whole community at odds. Finally there is the dull-witted, churlish fellow in whose mouth wisdom would be utterly out of place.*

There is always the problem of the sluggard, the lazy wretch whose badge is procrastination and somnolence. The persistence of this type of individual in Israel is demonstrated by the fact that attention is called to it twice (6:10; 24:33) in the very words uttered by the victim:

> A little sleep, a little slumber,
> A little folding of hands to rest.

* See further W. O. E. Oesterley, *The Book of Proverbs* (London, 1929), pp. lxxxiv–lxxxvii.

That, says the teacher, is the surest way to poverty and want. Hence he advises the learning of wisdom about the matter by observing the ways of the ant.

The vexing problem of unchastity is handled in a quite picturesque manner—by a verbal portrait of the adulteress and her sagacity and the tragedy in store for him who yields to her seduction. Proverbs 2:16–19 depicts the peril hidden beneath her attractiveness. Chapter 5 adds another dimension to the painting by stressing the disgrace involved for the hapless victim who falls for her evil charms, not to be undone by belated repentance. Connubial bliss with the wife of his youth is recalled. How blessed before deviation took place! Proverbs 6:20–35 contains a further admonition against the dire consequences of carnality. Perhaps the most graphic description in all literature of the moment of seduction, when the adulteress has inveigled her prey, is that given in chapter 7.

> My son, pay attention to my words
>   And keep in mind my commandments.
> Pay attention to my commandments and stay alive,
>   To my teachings as the apple of your eye.
> Tie them on your fingers,
>   Write them on the tablet of your heart.
> Say to wisdom, "You are my sister,"
>   And call insight your relative,
> To guard you against the harlot,
>   Against the carnal woman with her oily words.
> For through the window of my house,
>   Through my lattice I watched,
> And I noticed among the thoughtless ones,
>   I observed among the youths,
>   A lad without intelligence,
> Crossing the street at her corner,
>   Scampering on the way to her house,

In the twilight at eventide,
    At the fall of night and darkness.
And lo, a woman came to meet him,
    In the attire of a harlot, crafty in intent.
She is restless and excited,
    She cannot remain at home;
Now in the street, now at the plaza,
    She lies in wait around every corner.
And she grabs him and kisses him,
    With unblushing face says to him:
"I had my peace-offering obligations,
    And today I have paid my vows;
So I came out to meet you,
    To search for you, and I have found you.
I have prepared for my couch coverlets,
    Richly colored spreads of Egyptian linen.
I have sprayed my bed
    With myrrh, aloe scent, and cinnamon.
Come, let us have our fill of love till morning,
    Let us revel in love embraces,
For the man of the house is not at home,
    He has gone on a distant journey;
A purse of money he took with him
    And will return home at the full moon."
With her great persuasiveness she seduced him,
    With her oily lips she beguiled him.
In his credulity he follows after her,
    Like an ox going to the slaughter,
And like a deer lured into a snare

. . . .

Until an arrow rips into its liver;
    Like a bird plunging into a trap
Without knowing that its life is at stake.
And now, sons, listen to me
    And give attention to the words of my mouth.

Let not your heart detour to her ways,
   Do not turn aside into her paths.
How many are the victims she has brought down,
   How numerous all her slain!
Her house is the road to Sheol,
   Descending to the abode of death.

Finally there is the matter of intemperance in the use of intoxicating drink which afflicted people in the ancient world. Here is the text for many a temperance lesson:

Wine is a mocker,   strong drink a terrorizer;
Anyone misled by it   is not wise.
(Prov. 20:1)

And the most vivid and colorful portrait in all history of the drunkard is presented in 23:29–35:

Who has woe? Who has unsteadiness?
   Who has contentions? Who babbles?
Who has wounds without cause?
   Who has reddened eyes?
Those who linger over wine,
   Those who go repeatedly to try the blend.
Do not look on wine when it is red,
   When it sparkles in the glass.
It may glide down smoothly;
. . . .
Afterward it bites like a serpent
   And secretes [poison] like a viper.
Your eyes see astounding things,
   And your mind portrays crazy images.
You are like one reposing in the midst of the sea,
   Or like one slumbering on the top of a mountain.
They pommel me, but I feel no hurt,
   They strike me, but I don't feel it.
When shall I awake,
   That I may have another round!

Many other observations in Proverbs are equally timely and worthy of pondering—poverty and wealth, anger and scorn, bribery, niggardliness, suretyship, the tongue as a source for good or evil. Serious attention to and honest meditation upon the book of Proverbs might spare us many a heartache and help us to avoid innumerable pitfalls in the way of life.

THE MAN FROM UZ
(Job)

The book written about the man from Uz is a poem, a literary creation depicting the author's conception of the problem or problems raised by the experience of the leading character in a great life drama. That there was once a man from Uz is almost certain in view of the universality of the theme of the book and the fact that suffering is not an abstraction concocted by an over-fertile imagination. The history of Israel is, in some ways, the story of suffering, of persons and groups.

The name Job (*A-ia-ab* = "Where is the father") occurs in the Amarna Letters of the fourteenth century B.C. and several centuries before that in Egyptian and cuneiform texts dealing with Palestine and Syria. It is found in the Bible, apart from the present book, only three times (Ezek. 14:14, 20; Jas. 5:11); in the Ezekiel passages it is associated with the names Daniel and Noah. Daniel and Job as personal names are known outside the Bible and were current in Western Asia in the second millennium B.C. That does not mean that our hero was the person named in the inscriptions; it does indicate that the name was not fictitious.

The locale of Job is uncertain, but two traditions concerning it have come down to us. One places it in the Hauran. Genesis

10:23 makes Uz a son of Aram, and Josephus (*Antiquities* I.6.4) refers to a tradition according to which Uz was the founder of Trachonitis and Damascus. Another locates it somewhere in or around Edom. In Genesis 36:28 Uz is described as the son of Dishan who is grouped with the children of Seir, the Horite chiefs. In Genesis 22:21 Uz is said to be the eldest son of Nahor and, with a second son, Buz, represents the region connecting Aramaeans, Edomites and Arabians. Perhaps the provenance of our story was the old caravan route between Edom and the Hauran, for Job was a wealthy merchant prince like Abraham, though he was not an Israelite.

Content and Form

The poem of Job is a majestic drama depicting the experience of a great sufferer whose story is told in the prologue (1:1–3:1) which is in prose and does not antedate the sixth century. It reflects an Aramaic background. The original story, in all probability, goes back to the second millennium B.C. as the personal names show, but the present form falls somewhere between the ninth and seventh centuries, as demonstrated by the names of the friends, the reference to Chaldaean and Sabaean bandits, and the stage of thought developed in the poem itself. The conception of suffering here portrayed falls somewhere between the Babylonian texts which depict divine justice as inscrutable, demanding abject humility and self-abasement before the gods, and the Second Isaiah where suffering is regarded as vicarious (53:4–12).

Following the prologue is a series of three cycles of dialogues between Job and his friends prompted by the sufferer's complaint in 3:3–26:

May the day on which I was born perish,
  And the night that proclaimed, "A man child is conceived."
May the day be darkness,
    May God above not cherish it,
      Or light beam upon it.
May darkness and deathly gloom recover it,
    A cloud descend upon it,
      The darkening of the day frighten it.
That night—may thick darkness envelop,
    May it be excluded from the days of the year,
      Unreckoned among the number of months.
See, that night—may it be sterile,
    May no shouts of joy arise in it.
May the cursers of Yam curse it,
    Those who know how to curse Leviathan.
May the stars of its morning be darkness,
    Its hope for light non-existent,
      And may it not behold the eyelids of the dawn;
Because it did not shut the doors of my [mother's] womb
  And hide adversity from my eyes.
Why did I not die enwombed,
    Or issue forth from the belly and expire?
Why did the knees receive me,
    Or why the breasts, that I should suck?
For then I should have lain down and been still,
  I should have slept and thus had a resting place
With kings and world counselors
    Who build tombs for themselves,
Or with princes with gold,
    Who fill their houses with silver.
Or else hidden by miscarriage, I might indeed have come to be
  Like infants who never see the light!
There the wicked do not give trouble,
    The weary are at rest.
There prisoners are carefree together,
    They hear not the shout of the taskmaster.

> The small and the great are there,
> And the slave is free from his master.
> Why is light given to the careworn,
> And life to the embittered of spirit,
> Who long for death, but it comes not,
> Dig for it more eagerly than for hidden treasure,
> Who rejoice exceedingly
> And are cheered when they find the grave?
> Why is light given
> To the man whose way is hidden,
> Whom God has hemmed in on every side?
> For sighing precedes my meal,
> And my groanings flow out like water.
> For the fear I dread besets me,
> And the terror I contemplate befalls me.
> I am not at ease and I am not calm;
> I am not free from tension, because reverses keep coming.

Each of the cycles follows the same pattern. Each of the friends speak in the order of seniority and Job responds to each one immediately after he has finished. The final cycle is somewhat confused in the present text as the arguments become more acrimonious and less well ordered. The Elihu monologues (32–37) add little to the story; they were inserted later by an orthodox zealot who could not conceive of a situation with which traditional dogma could not cope. The highlight of the book is the first speech of the Lord (38:1–39:30), portions of which follow:

> Who, then, is this that confuses counsel
> By words without meaning?
> Gird up, now, your loins like a man,
> That I may interrogate you, that you may teach me!
> Where were you when I laid the foundation of the earth?
> Tell me, since you have the knowledge to do so!
> Who established its measurements?
> Speak out, if your intelligence is equal to it!

Have you ever in your life summoned the morning?
  Or regulated the appearance of the dawn,
That it should take hold of the ends of the earth,
  To shake out the wicked from it?
It turns itself like clay under a seal,
  And is tinted like a garment.
The wicked have their light withheld
  And their uplifted arm broken.
Have you gone to the fountains of the sea,
  Or wandered about the grounds of the deep?
Have the gates of death been disclosed to you,
  Or have you ever beheld the gates of darkness?
Have you ever comprehended the breadth of the earth?
  Speak out, now, if you know all this!
Can you bind the chains of the Pleiades,
  Or loose the bonds of Orion?
Are you familiar with the ordinances of heaven,
  Or can you impose their arrangements for earth?
Can you raise your voice to the clouds,
  To make them cover you with a swell of water?
Does the hawk soar by your insight,
  And spread his wings southward?
Does the eagle rise in flight at your word,
  When he builds his nest on high?

The epilogue (42:7–16) confirms the relative innocence of Job who is vindicated by the maintenance of his integrity and duly rewarded. The book, writes Paul Dhorme, "is not like a snowball that increases from the outside, but like a plant that grows from within."*

* *Le Livre de Job* (Paris, 1926), p. xlix.

The Arguments

The poetic portion of the drama begins with Job's lamentation of his lot. He complains bitterly about his condition, cursing the day of his birth, and questioning the justice of God who has fenced him in in his wretched state. He cannot escape. Job's outburst calls forth the first address of Eliphaz who reminds him that his fear of God (his religion) ought to be his assurance (4:6). After all he is just encountering what mortal man can expect (4:17). Job retorts rather sharply that instead of reproof he should be shown sympathy (6:14). Wherein has he sinned (6:24b), especially so greatly as to justify the torture that has befallen him? Job ends his reply to Eliphaz with a biting prayer to the afflicting God. Then Bildad takes the word, reaffirming the justice of God and the guilt of Job (8:1–10). God will not reject a perfect man. Experience proves that the godless are crushed (8:11–22). Job admits that a man cannot be right with God (9:1–10) who, however, is not limited by the moral law and hence destroys both the innocent and the guilty (9:11–35). Once more he appeals to God (10:1–22).

Zophar, the youngest of his friends, is less circumspect and more terse in his comments. Job is presumptuous in pleading his innocence, for he cannot fully know God or understand the obviously secret sins for which he is being punished (11:1–12). If he would only bethink himself and appeal to the Lord, his troubles would vanish (11:13–20). Job then chides his friends once more by protesting that while he suffers the manifestly wicked prosper (12:1–6). Let God prove him guilty (13:1–27). As things are, man is hopeless; he dies and it is all over (14:7–22).

In this cycle the interlocutors agree on certain points such as the transcendence, omnipotence and omniscience of God, but they clash on the application of his justice. The friends attempt to force his case into the mold of human justice which breaks down in this instance.

In the second cycle the addresses become more spirited and more rigorously logical. The points of antithesis are unchanged. In the third cycle, "The admirable peroration of Job ends with this protestation of innocence and this appeal to the supreme tribunal [ch. 31]. All the insinuations of his friends are reduced to the vanishing point. His misfortune is beyond description but it is not chastisement for sin, for Job himself maintains his faith in God and his justice and mercy for his fellowmen. Misfortune is a fact. So is innocence. The theories of Job's friends denied this contradiction, they never explained it. Job recognizes it, but he also explains it no further. The problem of the relationship between moral goodness and happiness, moral evil and unhappiness is not yet solved. The solution is still awaited" (Dhorme, *op. cit.*, p. xliii).

The Elihu speeches are more subtle than those of the other friends. He explores the meaning of sorrow and tribulation. He describes the ways in which divine justice operates. He envisages the case of Job only secondarily, although he frequently mentions him by name. He does not probe beyond the traditional religious view of confessing sin, returning to God, conversion.

The Yahweh discourses reaffirm the inscrutability of God, his power and majesty in creation, whose ways are past finding out. The problem raised by Job is not solved but Job submits in humility. He has the satisfaction of hearing the divine voice for which he clamored (13:3; 23:3–7). That gave him confidence that now he had the attention of heaven. There he was content to rest his case.

Conclusion

When all is said and done, the book of Job goes about as far as possible. There is profound mystery involved in adversity and suffering. One may regard it as the result of sin, as redemptive and disciplinary, but the "why" of suffering, together with the observable fact of its unequal distribution, remains as enigmatic as ever. Paul's dictum (Rom. 8:18) moves the trial court to heaven; it asserts but without explanation. The easy solutions so often announced usually come from those who, like the friends of our hero, are never on the same side of the fence (Job 16:4). It could be that the book of Job is not meant primarily to offer an apology for suffering but rather to illustrate the vindication of God's faith in the integrity of Job, a principle more fully exhibited in him who endured, without flinching, the cross of Calvary.

XXVI

THE NOTEBOOK OF A SKEPTIC
(Ecclesiastes)

Not the least of the virtues of the Old Testament lies in its ideas, attitudes and personal representatives from the whole gamut of life. Its thought soars to majestic heights in the Psalms and prophets and plunges to the depths in Job and Ecclesiastes. Unlike any other book of religion it records and reflects upon every aspect and condition of life because it deals with human thought and experience at every level. It glosses over nothing, it offers no propaganda except that of the relationship of Israel to God and as such speaks of blessings and curses, praises and blames, faithfulness and unfaithfulness, good and evil, devotion and skepticism.

Ecclesiastes has few parallels of similar extent in ancient religious treatises that have come down to us. Renan thought it was the only charming book ever written by a Jew. Heine called it "the canticles of skepticism," and Franz Delitzsch, one of the great Bible scholars of the nineteenth century, dubbed it "the canticles of the fear of God." It was the favorite book of Frederick the Great who saw in it "the mirror of princes."* President Kennedy frequently quoted from it.

* P. Haupt, *The Book of Ecclesiastes* (Baltimore, 1905), p. 1.

General Aspects of Qoheleth

Luther referred to Ecclesiastes as "the Preacher." It is easy to see how he got the idea from the Greek and Latin titles. The word Ecclesiastes is related to "ekklesia," the Greek word for assembly, and denominates one who sat in or spoke in the assembly. The Hebrew title is Qoheleth which Henry Cazelles has defined as "the man of the *qahal* (i.e., the congregation) who has charge of directing the holy community."* The term does not occur elsewhere in the Bible.

Just how the book came to bear that name is explained in the superscription: "The words of Qoheleth, son of David, king in Jerusalem." The person responsible for it attributed the book to Solomon, on the basis of I Kings 8:1, whose name bore great weight in the argument for canonicity. However, Qoheleth is a pseudonym and may have been deliberately enigmatic. The thought and language, together with such passages as 4:14; 10:4-5, demonstrate that Solomon was not the author. Ecclesiastes 12:9-11 describes the writer as a wise man and teacher; but further knowledge about him can only be gleaned from the thought patterns and reflections in his book. He appears to have resided in a cultural center such as Jerusalem, possibly in Alexandria. He was a teacher and counselor in his old age. He was acquainted with the upper classes of his community, though he himself may have been of humble birth. He was well-informed on history and the religious traditions of his people, and probably enjoyed the benefits of travel. He had no children of his own; he may even have been a bachelor. When he compiled his notebook he was an old man, a lover of life, justice and truth.

---

* H. Cazelles, "La titulature du roi David," *Mélanges bibliques rédigés en l'honneur de André Robert* (Paris, 1957), pp. 135 f.

Qoheleth must have lived and worked sometime early in the third century when Greek ideas were being disseminated in the eastern Mediterranean world but before Persian influence had waned as may be seen from the use of Persian words. One gets the impression from a close reading of his book that the author's knowledge of Greek thought was based on hearsay rather than on direct contact with Greek literature. Perhaps it accrued from his travels or from travelers passing through his own community. Aramaic characteristics abound and the Hebrew itself is late. Fragments of the book dating from the second century B.C. have been found at Qumran.

Reflections from the Notebook

One of the reasons for regarding the work of Qoheleth as a notebook is its composition. Like Proverbs it is made up of observations on subjects that occupied the writer's attention over a protracted period of time. Robert Gordis in *Koheleth, the Man and His World* (New York, 1955), has listed eighteen propositions, exclusive of the superscription and epilogue which are later additions. They are precisely the subjects pondered by an old man who had lived a fairly full life in a confused age, an age of transition.

It is impossible to discuss all of these subjects but it may be of some interest to consider a few of them and then present a summary statement of the theology of the author. One of the most characteristic observations of Qoheleth is that of the repetitiveness or perhaps uniformity of nature. To him there is no progress in the movements of the natural order. Generations come and go, the sun rises and sets in the same place every day, year in and year out rivers keep pouring their waters into the sea which is never full. From these endless cycles the conclusion is drawn that

> What has been will continue to be,
> And what has been done will continue to be done,
> And there is not a new thing under the sun.
> If there were something about which it can be said,
> "See here, this is new,"
> It was already present in the ages before us.
>
> (1:9–10)

Why do men think of things as new? It is because

> There is no recollection of former things;
> There will not even be remembrance of later things
> By those present at the very end.   (1:11)

It may be that the author wishes to direct attention to the uniformity and dependability of nature, while at the same time lamenting the fact of man's forgetfulness or his failure to be concerned about the lessons one generation could teach its successor. It may be a plea of the wise man for his readers to be instructed by the discipline of history. It appears that the Hebrew word usually translated "vanity" or "futility" ought to be rendered "incomprehensibility," in which case the writer expresses his inability to comprehend the regularity of nature and, more importantly, why man never seems to be able to profit from the experiences of the past.

Another interesting observation, somewhat akin to the one just mentioned, is the famous catalogue of appointed times and seasons in 3:1–15—a favorite passage of the late President Kennedy.

> Everything has its appropriate time, And there is a time for every purpose under the heavens:

A time to be born   and a time to die,
A time to plant   and a time to pull out what is planted,
A time to kill   and a time to heal,
A time to smash   and a time to build,
A time to cry   and a time to laugh,
A time to weep   and a time to dance,
A time to throw away stones   and a time to gather stones,
A time to embrace   and a time to keep from embracing,
A time to seek   and a time to spend,
A time to keep   and a time to throw away,
A time to tear   and a time to mend,
A time to be quiet   and a time to speak,
A time to love   and a time to hate,
A time for war   and a time for peace.

What profit then does the laborer derive from his work? I have observed the task God has laid upon men to be tormented with; he has made everything appropriate in its time. He has even invested them with perplexity,* so that man cannot comprehend the work God has done from beginning to end. I know there is nothing better than for them to be happy and do good so long as life lasts. Indeed, every person who eats, drinks, and enjoys all his work—that is a divine gift. I know that everything God does lasts forever—to it nothing can be added and from it nothing can be taken away, for God has designed things so that men should stand in awe of him. What has been, already is, and what is, already has been and God endeavors to recapitulate what is past.

Verse 11 is interpretive here—God has made everything appropriate in its time. The whole realm of life's activities has meaning only when set in perspective, that is when they are in

* Meaning of the original is very uncertain. The present rendition is conjectural and based on one possible interpretation of the context.

conformity with the ordered arrangements of God's plan in the universe. The reason the actions of men are often askew is due to ignorance which is the basic complaint of Qoheleth.

Finally, there is the classic portrait of old age (12:1–7), possibly drawn from the writer's own experience. The infirmities besetting those who have reached the twilight of life are described in a most unique way—for instance, the watchmen of the house (= hands and arms), the strong men (= the legs), the grinding maids (= the teeth), the ladies peering through the windows (= the eyes), the double doors into the street (= the lips), the blossoming almond tree (= gray head), the silver cord (= the cord of life), the golden bowl (= the bowl of life), the jar (= the jar of life), the snapping or breaking of which signifies death.

Some other subjects discussed are the failure of justice (3:16–4:3), the folly of toil (4:1–16), religious decorum (5:1–6), the futility of greed (5:10–6:9), ignorance (6:10–12), the good life (7:1–14), the golden mean (7:15–25), women (7:26–29), loyalty to the king (8:1–9), the shortcoming of retribution (8:10–9:3), the inadequacy of wisdom (9:13–10:1), successful virtues (10:2–11:6).

Theology

Other wisdom literature is more or less general in nature. Qoheleth is personal and represents the meditations of an individual, probably composed as a legacy to those coming after him, to instruct them on what to expect in life. His bequest may be summarized under four categories:

(1) The doctrine of God. Behind the order of the universe is God (3:11; 8:17; 11:5), who is responsible for the inexorable consummation of events (3:1–15; 7:13). Yet Qoheleth's God is not quite the personal, moral Yahweh of the rest of the Old Tes-

tament; he is more like a cosmic power. He is deistic (5:2). His activity is beyond comprehension (3:10–11; 8:17; 11:5). The homage paid to this God is due to fear (3:14–15; cf. 5:1–7; 7:18; 8:2).

(2) God's relationship to man. God is responsible for man's creation (12:7), the length of his days (5:18; 8:15; 9:12), his troubles (1:13; 3:10) and his joys (2:24, 26; 3:13; 5:19–20). The idea of retribution here (6:8; 8:10b, 14a) and hereafter (5:15–16; 6:6; 9:5; 10; 11:8; 12:7) is wanting. There is no future life (3:19–20; 12:7).

(3) God and nature. There is no progression in life or nature. Planets and seasons move in regularity (1:5–11), so do the generations of man (1:3–4). The evils in society come from God (3:10–15) or bad kings (3:16). There is only unrelieved oppression for the poor (5:8; 4:1; 8:9; 10:5–7).

(4) The future is unknowable (3:11, 22; 6:12; 7:14, 24; 8:7, 17; 10:14) and messianism incomprehensible (6:11). There is no resurrection (9:4–6, 10).

The skepticism with which Qoheleth has been charged may be somewhat of a misrepresentation. His notebook contains observations gathered from a long life. In the final analysis they may be more realistic than surface appearance warrants. The author does believe in the uniformity of nature and his conceptions, often predicated as incomprehensible, do reflect many mysteries not yet probed by man.

XXVII

THE HYMNBOOK OF ISRAEL
(Psalms)

No book of the Old Testament is so widely known and loved as that of Psalms. In his preface to the Psalms, Luther wrote:

> The Psalter is precious and dear because it holds out so clearly the promise involved in Christ's death and resurrection, and prefigures his kingdom and the posture and essence of the whole of Christianity that it may be called a little Bible in which everything that stands in the whole Bible is composed most beautifully and succinctly—a splendid enchiridion or handbook made to order. I really think the Holy Ghost has assumed the task of assembling a short Bible and pattern book of all Christianity or all saints so that whoever cannot read the whole Bible has here almost all of it gathered up in a small volume. . . . If you want to look at a portrait in miniature of the holy Christian Church in living color and form, take the Psalter where you have a splendid, bright, pure mirror that will show you what Christianity is. Yes, you will even find yourself there and the right "know yourself" (*gnothi seauton*), as well as God himself and all his creatures.*

Numerous hymns and songs appear elsewhere in the Bible, often in a specific historical context (e.g., Ex. 15; Deut. 32;

---

* *D. Martin Luthers Vorreden über die einzelnen biblischen Bücher und vermischte Aufsätze,* pp. 20–23.

Judg. 5; II Sam. 1). But in the present book of Psalms we have
an anthology of sacred songs compiled for use in the religious
services of the period of the Second Temple. Apparently many
were composed and used liturgically at the shrines of both kingdoms during the pre-exilic period.

The contents of the Psalter in its present form represents the
deposit of devotional and didactic poems covering a period of
nearly a thousand years. Many of the psalms were taken over
from Canaanite and other sources, not, of course, without being
made to conform with Israelite theology—and hence go back in
origin far into the second millennium B.C.

Psalmody continued even after the completion and canonization of the Psalter as may be seen from the Qumran scroll of
Thanksgiving Hymns and the New Testament. The Magnificat
(Luke 1:46–55), the Benedictus (Luke 1:68–79) and the Nunc
Dimittis (Luke 2:29–35) are psalms of the highest order. Then
there is the Logos hymn for the prologue of John's Gospel and
the dirge on the fall of Babylon (= Rome) in the book of Revelation (ch. 18), based largely on Ezekiel's requiem for Tyre
(chs. 26, 27).

> Alas! alas! thou great city,
> thou mighty city, Babylon!
> In one hour has thy judgment come.   (Rev. 18:10b)

> Alas! alas, for the great city
> that was clothed in fine linen, in purple and scarlet,
> bedecked with gold, with jewels, and with pearls!
> In one hour all this wealth has been laid waste.
>   (vss. 16, 17a)

> Alas, alas, for the great city
> Where all who had ships at sea grew rich by her wealth!
> In one hour she has been laid waste.   (vs. 19bc)

The Character of the Psalms

The Psalms are poems whose structure and form are only now becoming intelligible. Moreover, they are religious poems written to be accompanied by instruments when sung by persons whose hearts are in tune with God. They celebrate the relationship between the individual Israelite or the Israelite community and God on every level of experience. Not a facet of life is left untouched. Thus some of these sacred songs reflect the way of the Torah, some are reminiscent of the message of the prophets, some recall the ways and the power-filled acts of God in creation and history, and others are purely devotional. While all of them are fraught with Israel's conception of Yahweh her God, with theology, they are basically religious in character, that is, they have to do with man's response to God in the varied life and history of the nation. In a word, the Psalms are response literature.

The most striking impression made upon the reader of the Psalter is the diversity of experiences exhibited in almost every section, sometimes in a single psalm. A German scholar once wrote that the psalms are "words saturated with experience." As such they are the vehicle for the expression of diverse moods and sentiments occasioned by local circumstances or situations. There are praises and thanksgivings, lamentations and dirges, hymns of joy and exhilaration, paeans of victory and requiems of defeat.

It is precisely for that reason that the Psalms are so universal in application and use. Human feelings and dispositions produced by all sorts of life circumstances are pretty much the same now as when the Psalmists wrote. And we have no better medium for their expression than the words and phrases coined by Israel's great religious poets and singers.

The Use of the Psalms

Beginning with I Chronicles 16—where the constructed psalm is composed of Psalms 105:1–15; 96; 106:1, 47–48—increasing use appears to have been made of psalms in the worship life of the Hebrews. The earliest record so far of the Psalms as authoritative Scripture is I Maccabees 7:17 where Psalm 79:3 is quoted. The Qumran community had a psalmbook of its own—the well-known Hodayoth (= Songs of Thanksgiving or Praise)—whose individual songs contain many quotations from and reminiscences of our book of Psalms. According to the translators of the Revised Standard Version, there are quotations from or allusions to some eighty Psalms in seventeen books of the New Testament. Altogether there are about one hundred and eighty such quotations or allusions. Five passages are quoted ten or more times; fifty-four only once. These statistics point to a wide knowledge and significant appreciation of the Psalms by the several writers of the New Testament. The late J. P. Peters once wrote, "In the New Testament we find 'David' standing in authority and popular regard side by side with 'Moses' and 'the prophets.'" (*The Psalms as Liturgies* [London, 1922], p. 81.)

Familiarity with and use of the Psalms in the New Testament Church was due, in large measure, to the religious heritage of the early Christians. In Judaism, in New Testament times, there was, in all probability, a triennial cycle in the course of which the entire Pentateuch, sections from the prophets, and from the corresponding five books of the Psalter were read in Synagogue services.

From the Mishnah Tractate Tamid, which deals with daily

sacrifices, we learn about the use of some of the specific Psalms in Jewish worship. Psalm 24 was used on the first day of the week, Psalm 48 on the fifth day, Psalm 93 on the day before the Sabbath, Psalm 92 on the Sabbath, and Psalm 30 for the dedication of a home. The Egyptian Hallel (Pss. 113–118) was sung at Passover time, at the Feast of Weeks and at the Feast of Tabernacles.

Ignatius introduced antiphonal singing of the Psalms at Antioch about A.D. 100. Jerome speaks of farmers, vinedressers, shepherds and laborers pursuing their occupations with Psalms on their lips. Chrysostom says, "If we keep vigil in the Church, David comes first, last and midst." From the Church Fathers can be seen how the Psalms were used in worship. Sometimes they were sung by the congregation, sometimes by solo voices or as *cantus responsorius* (responsive song) or as *cantus antiphonalis* (antiphonal song).

The churches of the Reformation laid great stress upon Psalms as may be observed from the writings, sermons and commentaries of Luther and Calvin, their use in the Scottish Psalter, the Anglican Prayer Book and the Hymns of Wesley. To this day they occupy a prominent place in the liturgies of the Church, in responsive readings and in stately anthems. But perhaps most significantly, their forceful and expressive language has become the vehicle of public and private prayers of the devout adherents of the Jewish and Christian faiths.

Some Psalm Types

Many years ago Hermann Gunkel pointed out that there were three basic types of psalms as determined by their content and usage—hymns, songs of praise and thanksgiving, and songs of

complaint or lamentation. It may be of interest to treat briefly a
representative psalm of each of these types.

Illustrative of the first type is Psalm 8 which is hymnal in
character and whose theme is the Creator and his creation.

> O Yahweh, our Lord,
>> how majestic is your name
>> in all the earth!
>
> You have inscribed your splendor upon the heavens.
> By the mouth of infants and sucklings
>> you have laid a foundation of strength,
>>> on account of your adversaries,
>>>> to put to silence the enemy and avenger.
>
> When I gaze at your heavens,
>> the product of your fingers,
>>> the moon and the stars you have fixed there—
>
> What is a man that you should think of him,
>> or a human being that you should take note of him?
>
> Yet you have made him little less than God,
>> and you have crowned him with glory and majesty;
> You have made him ruler over the product of your hands,
>> You have put everything at his disposal—
>
> All sheep and oxen,
>> even the cattle of the field,
>>> the birds of the air and the fish of the sea,
>>>> as well as the commerce of the seas.
>
> O Yahweh, our Lord,
>> how majestic is your name
>> in all the earth!

The psalmist was profoundly impressed by a contemplation
of the elemental things of the world—the splendorous heavens
with its planets on the one hand and the potential of infants

and sucklings on the other. These all reminded him of the majesty, thoughtfulness and power of the Creator God who in his unfathomable wisdom had made them all. The more he thought about them the more he was overwhelmed by the mystery of the stellar universe and the origin and significance of human life. Like the Königsberg philosopher Immanuel Kant, he stood in awe of the star-lit heavens above him, and the teeming life of little children. Both were so mysterious, so wonderful, and so new every night and day. For a moment he was struck by the apparent insignificance of man as he moved about under the incalculably enormous canopy of the sky. But his thoughts were soon lifted up once more when he recalled that man too came from the mighty hand that had wrought the wondrous universe around and above him. He was invested with a creaturely dignity and bore the stamp of the Creator. He was little less than God, for he had been endowed with the power of procreation and charged with dominion over the other creatures of earth. He was, in a sense, lord of earth. Hence he voiced his paean of praise to Yahweh, the majestic God of heaven and earth who was the Author of all—for man. What an honor conferred upon him! What an awesome responsibility—to be ruler over the product of God's hand! That called for the highest praise and the summoning of all his God-given energy and means to glorify the Lord, as David expressed it in I Chronicles 29:10–19.

A good example of the psalms of thanksgiving is Psalm 32:

Fortunate is the man whose burden of guilt has been lifted,
  Whose sin has been blotted out.
Fortunate is the man against whom Yahweh does not reckon transgression,
  And in whose spirit is no thought of deception.
When I kept silent my very bones creaked

With my outcry throughout the day.
For day and night your hand lay heavy upon me,
     My energy was exhausted,
          As by dehydration in summer.

I disclosed my sin to you,
     And my iniquity I did not conceal.
I said, "I will confess my evil deeds to Yahweh,"
     And you lifted the burden of my sin.
For this reason let every devoted person pray to you,
     When you alone may be found;
In the flood of many waters,
     They will not touch him.
You are my covert,
     From distress you preserve me,
          with joyful shouts of deliverance you surround me.

I will teach you and direct you
     In the way you must go;
          I will provide counsel, with my eye upon you.
Do not be like the horse or mule,
     That resist bridle and bit;
          Approached for harnessing,
               It will not come near you.

Many are the pains of wrongdoers,
     But he who trusts in Yahweh,
          Covenant love surrounds him.

Rejoice in Yahweh and be jubilant, O righteous ones,
     Shout for joy all you who are right-thinking.

The poet had experienced an inner release from tension and
anxiety in the wake of confession of sin which issued in divine
forgiveness. Before that he was bent low, like Bunyan's Christian, with an intolerable burden. He was utterly exhausted, men-
tally confused and spiritually bankrupt. But when he came

boldly, openly and unabashedly before Yahweh with the full disclosure of his condition, the situation changed completely. Yahweh unleashed his burden, removed it far from him, and became his refuge, guide and teacher. Then he became a truly happy person. On the basis of his experience he now is ready to give direction and advice to all who will listen. More than that, he summons all righteous and rightly-disposed persons to give thanks to Yahweh and rejoice in his marvelous goodness.

Psalm 70 is categorized as a song of complaint. There are many such psalms in the Psalter, mostly individual in character (e.g., Pss. 3, 5, 22, 28, 31, 42, 43, 51, etc.). This Psalm is also a portion of Psalm 40, where it forms the conclusion to a thanksgiving song.

> O God deliver me,
>   O Yahweh act quickly on my behalf.
>
> Let those who seek my life
>   Be put to shame and be abashed.
>
> Let those who desire my ruin
>   Be turned back and be dishonored.
>
> Let those who say, "Aha, Aha,"
>   Be dismayed because of their shame.
>
> May all who seek you
>   Be glad and rejoice in you.
>
> May those who cherish your salvation
>   Say continually, "God is great."
>
> I am meek and poor;
>   Hurry to me, O God.
>
> You are my helper and my refuge.
>   O Yahweh, do not delay!

The writer finds himself in a desperate situation. His life is in grave peril. Enemies threaten him from every side and appear to be closing in on him. There is nowhere to turn except to Yahweh to whom he appeals in utmost haste. He pleads that somehow God will turn back his oppressors, stay them before they work their way on him. Moreover, he asks that the enemies be brought before the bar of public knowledge so that their shameful acts may be exposed. The violent impatience of the psalmist illustrates the common human characteristic of excitability when one is confronted by forces with which he cannot easily cope. But, like the psalmist, in the second wind of faith he is moved to call upon the Lord because he alone is sufficient, for he is great.

XXVIII

THE WAY OF LOVE
(Canticles)

Agur, son of Jakeh of Massa,* in one section of his proverbs, confesses that among the four things he cannot understand is that of "the way of a man with a maiden" (Prov. 30:19d). That is what Canticles, or The Song of Songs, or The Song of Solomon is about. It is the only purely "secular" collection of poems in the Bible. Needless to say, the Hebrews did not have the same conception of the secular and the religious aspects of life that obtains in the Western world, as may be seen from their writings. Hence the appearance of a series of such compositions as these in their literature is not surprising.

Later generations, with a more developed sense for what we would refer to as the more specifically religious, had their qualms about the presence of Canticles in the canon of Sacred Scripture. But the name of Solomon (1:1, 5; 3:7, 9; 8:12), references to the king (1:4, 12), and the allegorical interpretation of the entire complex of writings, according to which the lover was equated with the Lord and the beloved with Israel, overcame whatever caveats had been raised against canonization. The prevailing view of the Rabbis was stated forcefully by Rabbi Akiba:

* Apparently a North Arabian tribe.

"No Israelite ever disputed the canonicity of the *Song of Songs*. No day in all the history of the world is as worthy as the one in which the *Song of Songs* was given to Israel, for all the Scriptures are holy, but the *Song of Songs* is the most holy" (Mishnah Yadayin 3/5). Moreover, an argument in its favor was the frequent reference to Israel as the bride of Yahweh (see the figures employed in Hos. 2; Jer. 2:2; 3:20; etc.).

Composition

Nineteenth-century scholars began to interpret the book literally and saw in it a love drama with two (Franz Delitzsch) or three (Heinrich Ewald) characters. Some years ago Leroy Waterman* divided it into two parts. The first one, he thought, depicts a scene in the Jerusalem harem of the king in which the participants were a chorus, Solomon, a group of court ladies composed of queens and concubines, and a girl servant from Shunem. The second one centers about the hamlet of Shunem and has three characters: the brothers of the girl, her lover and the girl herself.

New evidence from outside sources—notably from Egypt—has been produced in the last few decades and has led scholars and interpreters to a better understanding of what Canticles really is. They have come to see that it is a concatenation of love songs of varied length celebrating the deepest passion of the human heart. Some of them may be marriage songs (cf. also Ps. 45), while others are simply erotic poems whose specific theme is determined by the experience or inspiration of the moment.

Robert Gordis** thinks the Song of Songs is composed of twenty-nine love poems. As such it is somewhat analogous to a

* *The Song of Songs* (Ann Arbor, 1948).
** *The Song of Songs* (New York, 1954).

collection of Egyptian love poems dating from the Twentieth Dynasty (ca. 1200–1085 B.C.) that consists of a series of seven cantos ("houses"), in which two lovers praise and extol each other. In three of them the youth (called the brother) sings to his beloved; in the other four the maiden (called the sister) addresses her lover in extravagant terms. Here is Canto vii in which the lover bewails his lovesickness for his beloved:

Seven days it is from yesterday that I have not seen the sister,
And sickness has crept upon me,
And I am become all heavy in my limbs,
And am forgetful of mine own body.
If the master-physicians come unto me,
My heart hath no comfort (of) their remedies;
The magicians, no resource is in them;
My sickness is not discerned.
That which I have said, behold it is what reviveth me,
Her name is that which can raise me up.
The coming and going of her messengers,
Is that which reviveth my heart.
More beneficial unto me is the sister than any remedies,
More important is she unto me than the entire compendium of
    medicine,
My salvation is her coming in from without,
When I see her, then am I well;
Openeth she her eye, then my limbs become young again;
Speaketh she, then I am strong,
And when I embrace her, she banisheth evil from me,
But she hath gone from me for seven days.*

In the eighth century A.D., Mamun, the son of Khalif Harun

---

* Quoted from *The Chester Beatty Papyri, No. I,* by Alan H. Gardiner (London, 1931), by permission of the Librarian of The Chester Beatty Library, Dublin.

al-Rashid, improvised, on the spur of the moment, a love poem in exchange for a beautiful slave girl of his father's.

> I kissed her from afar, a fair gazelle.
> And with my eyes I told her all my heart.
> She frowned me nay—I knew she wished me well
> By that quick smile which oped her lips apart.
> I paid my court as warmly as could be,
> Nor left that room till she belonged to me.*

The book of Canticles seems, then, to be nothing more or less than an anthology of the most exquisite and priceless love lyrics dating from the Solomonic age to the Persian period. It affords a valuable insight into a significant phase of Hebrew life and experience.

Some Themes

All sorts of subjects having to do with love, courtship and marriage appear here. Indeed few features of Hebrew life dealt with by biblical writers have been so fully and freely treated. Often the language seems rather suggestive, even crude, but then that is the way matters were handled in the world out of which Canticles came. As elsewhere, Hebrew writers here were concerned primarily with depicting the situation as it was. They did not attempt to gloss over what might appear inappropriate to us, or polish the description of their life experiences with polite and innocuous words.

The ornate language employed by the lovers in Canticles to commend each other is characteristic of every generation. The youth compares his sweetheart to "a mare of the chariot of

* Quoted by Sir John B. Glubb, *The Empire of the Arabs* (London, 1963), p. 317. Used by permission of Sir John B. Glubb.

Pharaoh," her eyes are "doves," her "hair is like a flock of goats," her "lips are like a scarlet thread," her "temples are like pomegranate slices," her "neck like the tower of David," "her two breasts like two fawns." In fact she is indescribably beautiful, without blemish.

The maiden's adoration of her lover is couched in equally grandiloquent descriptives. He is like "a sack of myrrh," "a bunch of henna." He is beautiful and sweet, her paramour to whom she pledges her love and vows to preserve herself for him alone.

The quality of human love is, of course, set forth in mundane language because that is the only way even the most deeply emotional and spiritual feelings can be expressed. One always has the impression, when talking about such profound matters, that more remains unsaid than said. Even the exalted poetry of the Song of Songs is inadequate to convey the essence of true love. The authors deal with the subject of love realistically, not abstractly.

We can grasp fully what impulses moved the maiden to exclaim, "I am lovesick" and "his ensign over me is love." And who has not experienced or observed the invitation to love in the springtime when nature bursts forth with new life and the air is filled with the fragrance of flowers!

> Lo, the winter is past,
> The rain is over and gone,
> The flowers appear on the earth,
> The time for singing has arrived.
> The voice of the turtledove is heard in our land,
> The fig tree puts forth its green figs,
> The vines blossom and emit fragrance.
> Arise, come away, my love,
> My beautiful one, come away.   (2:11–13)

Many lovers have, no doubt, had the same disturbing dream related by the girl in 3:1-5. She dreamed of separation from her lover, for whom she called in vain. She searched the streets without success. In desperation she appealed for help to the watchmen, again without avail. Suddenly she spied him, sprang to him with open arms. Securely in her caresses, she held him fast and would not let go of him until he was lodged in her mother's house. In another poem one can almost hear the pounding heart of the maiden as she hastens to open the door for her lover (5:2), but, alas, while she was busy making herself presentable, he gave up knocking and left in despair. Undaunted she rushed through the city streets in pursuit of him, despite suffering personal humiliation at the hands of the police, driven on relentlessly in her search by the contemplation of his attractiveness and comeliness (5:10-16).

Illustrations

The overwhelming drive of love animating the heart of the young girl who idolizes her lover could not be more forcefully expressed than in the following verses:

> Let him kiss me with the kisses of his mouth,
> For your darling love is better than wine!
> The scent of your ointments is pleasant,
> Like oil poured out is (the fragrance of) your presence,
> Therefore do the maidens love you.   (1:2-3)

How picturesque the noble metaphors used in an attempt to describe the mutual admiration of the youthful lovers! Surely they awaken fond memories in most thoughtful and responsive readers.

> Girl — I am (like) a rose of Sharon,
>   A lily of the valleys.

Boy — Like a lily among briars,
  Is my sweetheart among (other) girls.

Girl — Like an apple tree among the trees in the forest
  Is my dear among (other) boys.
  I delight to sit in its shade,
  And its fruit is sweet to my taste. (2:1–3)

Reference to the palpitating hearts of true lovers recalls familiar feelings. The most satisfying and delightful things of life pale into insignificance when compared with the offerings of love.

You have made my heart throb, my sister, (my) bride,
You have made my heart throb with one (wink) of your eyes,
With one strand of your necklace.
How marvelous is your darling love,
How much more thrilling is your darling love than wine,
The scent of your ointments than any perfume.
Your lips, (my) bride, drip comb honey,
Honey and milk are under your tongue,
The scent of your garments is like the scent of Lebanon.
          (4:9–11)

The following verses comprise the most precious and powerful description of love in all literature. What could be more profoundly religious than the love that holds together two lives "till death doth them part"?

Put me like a seal upon your heart,
Like a seal upon your arm;
For love is powerful as death,
Passion as mighty as Sheol;
Its flames are (like) flames of fire,
A divine blaze.
Many waters cannot put out love,
Or rivers flood it away.
Should one offer to exchange the family treasures for love,
People would utterly despise him.   (8:6–7)

XXIX

A NEW BEGINNING
(Chronicles, Ezra, Nehemiah)

The destruction of Jerusalem by the Babylonians in 587 B.C. ended the existence of the Jewish state religion until the Maccabean period. Though hope was not abandoned for eventual restoration, as may be seen from the prophecies of Jeremiah (e.g., 29:4–15; 31:38–40; 32:15; 33:1–26) and Second Isaiah, the subsequent history of the Jewish people proves that the new Israel took a far different form from that which obtained in the pre-exilic period. Perhaps that was to be expected after the new covenant pronouncement of Jeremiah (31:27–34) and the soaring oracles of the great prophet of the Exile.

It was clear from the start that any impetus toward reconstruction would have to come from the community in exile, since all the competent scholars, priests and people were carried to Babylon in the course of three deportations (Jer. 52:28–30). The period of reconstruction began with Cyrus' conquest of Babylon in 539 B.C. and the rescript he issued a year later for the return of those Jews who were willing to do so (II Chron. 36:22–23; Ezra 1:1–4).

Those who responded to the invitation of Cyrus found conditions in the erstwhile homeland deplorable. The first step toward rebuilding a new religious structure was the erection of an altar (Ezra 3:2) and the reinstitution of sacrifices (Ezra 3:3–6). Following that the foundation of the Temple was laid (Ezra 3:7–13). Further building plans were interrupted or delayed by local complications inspired by "the people of the land" (i.e., those who filled the vacuum created by the exile of landholders in the course of the debacle some five or six decades earlier).

Ever since the events of 587 B.C. the territory of Judah was under foreign control, first of the Babylonians, now of the Persians. It became part of the province "Across the River" which was governed by a satrap. One of the districts of the province was Samaria where a local governor held sway. By virtue of the infiltration noted above, he claimed jurisdiction also over Judah, though the latter had never been officially assigned to Samaria. It would appear that Sheshbazzar,* and later his successor, Zerubbabel,** was more or less the recognized governing authority for the Jews.

That was bound to create trouble for the *golah* who were, at the outset, confronted by the syncretists who claimed a portion in the religious developments about to be undertaken at Jerusalem. The syncretists were the members of the communities surrounding Judah under the leadership mainly of Sanballat, the governor of Samaria, and Tobiah, the governor of Ammon. The Samaritans of the time were a mixed group composed of descendants of the more progressive elements of Israelites left in the

---

* Sheshbazzar (I Chron. 3:18) was the fourth son of King Jehoiachin and was apparently the first governor of Judah after the Exile (after 538 B.C.).
** Zerubbabel (I Chron. 3:19) was a grandson of King Jehoiachin and succeeded his uncle as governor of Judah. He was in office during the rebuilding of the Temple (520–516 B.C.).

land after the destruction of Samaria in 722 B.C. and the peoples
of other lands settled there by the Assyrians from time to time
(cf. Ezra 4:2). They were Yahwists but were no longer regarded as pure in race or religion. But farseeing exponents of the
religion of the fathers saw at once the danger to that religion in
such a move. During the exile in Babylon even some of the
best of the people were apparently lured away from the faith or,
at best, became indifferent. Those who returned were determined to rebuild not simply the institutions of their religion but
to keep themselves pure from any foreign or syncretistic influences. That purpose is what provoked the century-long conflict
with their neighbors in the homeland.

The struggles that took place between the orthodox Jews seeking to prevent a watering down of their ancestral faith and the
Samaritan community with its baneful influences and effects
are reflected in the books of Haggai, Zechariah and Malachi,
and in the books of Ezra and Nehemiah.

Historical Developments

To judge by the strictures of Malachi (first half of the fifth
century B.C.) there was a general moral collapse which may have
been due to internal troubles. Despite the completion of the
Second Temple in about 516 B.C. and, presumably, the func-
tioning of the cultus there seemed to be no overwhelming sense
of the full demands of Yahwism. Religious lethargy had taken
hold of the little community. There was no deep feeling of dedication to the Lord and there appears to have been only nominal
or perfunctory allegiance to him. The political machinations of
the time and locale may have been partly responsible for conditions. The people were at the mercy of hostile forces with
which they were too weak to cope. And there were few, if any,

rallying centers such as the priestly or prophetic voices of an earlier day.

Yet there were evidently some persons or groups who were concerned enough to be actively engaged in an endeavor to redeem the time. One of these groups may have sought to explore ways of remedying the situation by sending a delegation to the seat of the Persian government at Susa (Shushan), the ancient capital of Elam. It is also possible that the members of the delegation were on some other official business or visitors to their brethren in the Diaspora, though it is unlikely that they would have traveled so far for a merely social visit. In any event, Nehemiah, the cupbearer—a very important official in the Persian Court—inquired from them about conditions at Jerusalem. What he heard was depressing indeed: "The survivors who remained there in the province after the captivity are in dire straits and in disgrace; the wall of Jerusalem remains broken down and its gates ruined by fire" (Neh. 1:3). His reaction was quick and decisive. After laying the matter before the Lord in prayer, he requested from the king a leave of absence from his position at the royal court in order to go to Jerusalem to rebuild the city of his fathers.

Provided with a royal firman, Nehemiah made his way to Judah where, after an inspection tour of the walls, he immediately summoned the people to the task of rebuilding the walls of Jerusalem. It was clear to him that no stable community could be established until there was some measure of personal security and the people were freed from outside interference. The gigantic operation of reconstruction required careful organization and planning (Neh. 3), together with an iron will and determination on the part of leader and community. In time a new community spirit arose, for Nehemiah was able to infect many of the local elders, priests and artisans with renewed zeal for the enterprise so dear to his heart (4:6).

But not all was peace and harmony. Problems arose from within and without. Opposition from within threatened to disrupt the work. Certain shysters took advantage of their brethren and virtually enslaved them (Neh. 5). From the other side, Nehemiah and his fellow workers were confronted by the overt and covert acts of Sanballat, Tobiah and Geshem (Neh. 6), and their henchmen.

So persistent were the opponents of Nehemiah and so dispirited the community in general that he soon realized that external measures were insufficient in themselves to maintain order or make for the progress and growth of the commonwealth. Being a layman, he could not institute specifically religious reforms, but as governor he did have considerable authority which enabled him to exercise some control over certain aspects of the community's life. During his absence from Jerusalem, local forces of control surrendered to expediency so that when he returned (ca. 433 B.C.) he found things pretty much in confusion (13:6–9). He acted with dispatch—Tobiah was expelled from his room in the Temple, the Levites restored to their positions (13:10–14), sabbath regulations enforced (13:15–22) and the first step taken to purge the community of foreign vestiges (13:23–27).

The Work of Ezra

There is some uncertainty about the exact time when Ezra, who was probably the Chronicler, came to Jerusalem. Some scholars hold that he came in the seventh year of Artaxerxes I's reign (458 B.C.), in which case he would have preceded Nehemiah by about thirteen years (Ezra 7:7; Neh. 2:1). Others think his mission fell in the seventh year of Artaxerxes II's reign (398

B.C.), which would mean that he followed Nehemiah. The sequence of events is such that Ezra indeed seems to have come after Nehemiah, or at least that he was contemporary with the second visit of the latter.

It appears to the writer that the whole complex situation is best explained by supposing that Nehemiah's work of the reconstruction of the walls of Jerusalem and the establishment of external order and comparative security from hostile elements in surrounding areas proved inadequate by themselves to produce the stable, progressive and dynamic community he envisioned. He soon realized, devout layman that he was, that material organization was not enough. "Man cannot live by bread alone." The community had to be "enspirited," inspired, compelled by other resources. Motivation had to come from outside, from another direction, as the prophets of an earlier age had asserted. Nor could any sort of compromise with the syncretistic elements in the land be tolerated. The most heroic measures were called for if the faith of the fathers was to persist.

Here is where Ezra the scribe fits into the picture. He had been active in Jewish religious circles in Babylon for a long time. He was concerned particularly with the worship tradition of his people and was a serious student of the Law of Moses (Ezra 7:6), which was doubtless our present Pentateuch. His aim in coming to Judah was "to conduct an investigation about Judah and Jerusalem in harmony with the law of your God" (Ezra 7:14). The royal rescript called for the offering of sacrifices, the conduct of other cultic ceremonies and abundant provision from the royal treasuries for whatever was required in the service of the Lord (7:12–26).

The new beginning for Judah demanded a complete reorientation of the cult of the Lord which meant a reassessment of the history of Israel from a religious standpoint rather than from a political one as was the case in the work of the Deuteronomist whose great history (Deut. to II Kings) was compiled for the purpose of saving the nation from disaster. But the nation was no more. The territory of Judah was now part of a foreign state. As Ezekiel foresaw (chs. 40–48), the time had come to shift from a church state to a church, a movement undoubtedly begun in Babylon. The Temple had been rebuilt (516 B.C.) and the subprovince of Judah fairly well established. Nevertheless, no prophetic powers were necessary to see that the Jews could not reorganize themselves on the same basis as before the Exile.

The new beginning was consummated in the work of Ezra whose chief purpose was so to orient the religion of the Jews that they would not be syncretized out of existence. To that end he furnished them with fresh dynamic so as to operate within the physical and political context of the age. In his history (I and II Chronicles) he incorporated various genealogical lists to show the pure ancestry of each family and the legitimacy of Levitical and priestly lines, and endeavored to trace each back to its source. That was quite important from his point of view, for true Judaism must be based on purity from contamination of any kind. Hence it was not a matter of pride to insist on legitimate descent; it was a case of survival. On such a community composed of Jews who could prove their family connections with Abraham and his descendants so much would depend, the very existence of Judaism and its daughter, Christianity.

The Concerns of the Chronicler

For the Chronicler (Ezra?), the drive for the preservation of Judaism centered about three phases of its essential character. First, there was the stress on the Temple whose origin was connected with David. It was Israel's great king in whose heart was born the desire for a structure that would symbolize the presence of the Lord with his people and his concern for them. Although David did not actually build the Temple, he did make extensive preparations for the project (I Chron. 22:1–16), and left detailed plans for its construction by his son Solomon (I Chron. 28:1–21). The line of David, by the time of Ezra, had achieved a messianic status and to accentuate the temple plans and commands of the king would not only carry great weight but would lend authority to the purposes and needs of the day. Post-exilic Judaism was anchored in the institutions of religion and, consonant with contemporary beliefs, required both precedent and divine command (I Chron. 28:19) for its direction. For that reason so much was made of the Davidic plans for the Temple and their execution by Solomon. No less than thirteen chapters in Chronicles are devoted to the Temple. In addition to these, there are frequent references to temple cleansings (e.g., in the reigns of Joash, Hezekiah and Josiah).

Along with the Chronicler's concern for the Temple went his conception of the cultus—of worship in the Temple. His exalted view of the central sanctuary required a well-conceived and well-organized personnel. To that end there had to be priestly and Levitical functionaries meticulously structured and whose status according to family descent was without question.

There must be priests whose functions were carefully defined —they were the official trumpeters (I Chron. 16:6; Ezra 3:10, etc.), they ministered in the inner sanctuary (II Chron. 5:14; 29:16), they offered sacrifices on the altar (II Chron. 29:21), handled the blood of the paschal offering (II Chron. 30:16; 35:11), burned incense (II Chron. 26:18) and served as instructors of *torah* (= law) (II Chron. 15:3; 17:8).

The Levites were given special status and duties—they were the bearers of the Ark (I Chron. 15:15), singers (I Chron. 15:16–22) and gatekeepers (I Chron. 15:23). On occasion they could perform priestly duties (cf. II Chron. 29:5–11), or function as judges (II Chron. 19:8, 11), prophets (II Chron. 20:14), royal officials (I Chron. 26:20–30), temple janitors (II Chron. 29), fund collectors (II Chron. 24:5–11; 34:9) and construction foremen (II Chron. 34:12–13).

Finally came the temple servants (*nethinim*) whose appointment was traced to David (Ezra 8:20). They were the lowest order of temple officials (Neh. 7:73) and assisted the Levites (Ezra 8:20). They were separately housed in Ophel (Neh. 3:26, 31) or lived in separate sections in the cities of the Levites (Neh. 11:3).

All of these groups were believed to have been organized by David for cultic services. So far as the Chronicler is concerned, David was the father of temple worship and the founder of the various guilds that were established for its conduct. He was particularly anxious that worship personnel be of the right character and properly appointed so that the conduct of religious rites would be in accord with the requirements of the Lord. He wanted, at all cost, to avoid the perilous ways of the past and to maintain the holy relationship between the Lord and the congregation of Israel so that the covenant community might be the Lord's delight and that it, in turn, might enjoy his favor (Neh. 9:13–15).

It has often been pointed out that the Deuteronomist was strongly influenced by the preaching of the eighth-century prophets, many of whose ideas he incorporated into his work. Superficial impressions of the Chronicler might appear to negate them in favor of the priestly aspects of the religion of Israel. But a closer reading of his books demonstrates that he has not neglected the prophets. In fact, he refers to them more often than the Deuteronomist does.

The Chronicler not only mentions all of those whose names appear in Samuel and Kings, but five others. Moreover, he frequently speaks of books or collections of the oracles of prophets (no less than a dozen such references occur in I and II Chronicles), he attributes prophetic oracles to priests (II Chron. 24:20) and Levites (II Chron. 20:14–17), and refers to members of the musical orders as seers (Heman, I Chron. 25:1, 5; Asaph, II Chron. 29:30; Jeduthun, II Chron. 35:15). Prophetic oracles are interpreted as commands (II Chron. 29:25; Ezra 9:11) but nearly all of them are lacking in specifically moral content (in contradistinction from those recorded by the Deuteronomist in Samuel and Kings). They are devoted, by and large, to cultic matters or the law of equivalent returns (cf. II Chron. 12:5).

Summary

Thus it is clear that the Chronicler's concern is for a new Jewish community centering about the Temple and the cultic services connected with it. His history was intended to show how Israel prospered and enjoyed the blessings of the Lord when it remained true to him, in undivided loyalty, and rejected every vestige of syncretism. All its troubles, on the other hand, were due to deviation from the Lord, and its failure to observe proper cultic arrangements.

If the new community was to succeed it would have to remain pure. Its members would have to divest themselves of all foreign elements. They would have to reject participation in worship of Samaritans, Ammonites and Arabians, even put away the foreign wives who had been taken for practical purposes of expediency. This might be the last opportunity for the people of the covenant. To that end Ezra offered the struggling Jews in Judah and Jerusalem a new beginning with promises and warnings (Neh. 9:6–37). On their part, the several groups pledged their co-operation in making the community what he thought it should be.

The rest of the people, the priests, the Levites, the gatekeepers, the singers, the temple slaves, and all those who had separated themselves from the peoples of the land to the law of God, together with their wives, their sons, their daughters, and all those who had [reached the age of] discretion joined their worthy brethren in a solemn oath to follow the law of God transmitted through Moses the servant of God, and to observe and act in accordance with all the commands of Yahweh our Lord, with his judgments and his statutes. We will not give our daughters in marriage to the peoples of the land nor allow our sons to take their daughters in marriage; we will not buy from them on the sabbath or holy days the wares or any grain which the peoples of the land might bring on the sabbath day to sell, and that we will forego [the produce] of the seventh year and the exaction of any debt therein. Moreover we obligated ourselves to contribute one third shekel yearly for the service of the house of our God—for the layer bread, for the continual meal offering, for the continual burnt offering, the sabbaths, the new moons, festivals, and consecrated [gift] offerings and the sin offerings to atone for Israel, and for all the work of the house of our God. We determined by lot the supply of wood which the priests, the Levites and the people by families, at the appointed times year by year, were to bring to the house of our God to burn upon the altar of Yahweh our God, as prescribed in the law. We further obligated ourselves to bring in yearly the first fruits of our land and the first fruits of all our orchards to the house of Yahweh, and in addition thereto bring in the first-born of our sons and our cattle, as prescribed in the law,

and the first-born of our herds and our flocks to the house of
our God for the priests who minister in the house of our God.
We will bring also the choicest of our dough, our contributions,
and of the fruit of every tree, of wine and of oil to the priests
in the chambers of the house of our God, and the tithe of the
land to the Levites—the Levites are the ones who are to collect
the tithes in all our cult cities: the Aaronite priest must accom-
pany the Levites when they collect the tithes and the Levites
must take up a tithe of the tithes to the house of our God, to
the chambers of the treasury, for the Israelites and the Levites
must bring the produce of grain, wine and oil to those chambers
where the vessels of the sanctuary, the ministering priests, the
gatekeepers, and the singers are. We will not neglect the house
of our God.   (Neh. 10:28–39)

DENOUEMENT
(Daniel)

The Jews of the post-exilic period were no different, basically, from their brethren of other periods. They were perhaps somewhat more concerned, on the whole, about their faith, not just because of what transpired in the sixth century but rather because of the exigencies of their own situation. In the late Persian period, as subsequently, they were surrounded by hostile forces that undoubtedly led many to question whether the course they were pursuing was the right one. Were the deprivations and hardships really worth-while? Would the sufferings now be commensurate with coming glories for them or their children? Could they possibly be deluding themselves in their reliance upon the God of the fathers?

History

Amid the changing scenes of world empire, the condition of the Palestinian Jews became increasingly acute. Their lot in the closing years of Persian hegemony could hardly have been enviable. The refractory Samaritan community continued down to the time of Alexander the Great and after.

Under Artaxerxes II (404–358 B.C.) there occurred an uprising of western satraps of the Persian empire which was joined by Egypt which had successfully revolted around 401 B.C. However, trouble in Egypt in the fifth decade of the fourth century brought an end to that movement, and Persia, under Artaxerxes III (358–338 B.C.), recovered temporarily when the Nile province was reconquered (ca. 342 B.C.). Yet the death knell for Persia had already sounded as may be seen from the violent death of Artaxerxes Ochus and the ruthless poisoning of his son, Arses (338–336 B.C.), together with the slaying of his entire family. Darius III (336–331 B.C.) was the last Achaemenid king. He was defeated by Alexander at Arbela in 331 B.C. and world events entered upon another course.

The shift from Persian to Greek rule appears to have been accepted by the Jews without much resistance but the consequences of that change in the course of history were more far-reaching than they could have anticipated.

After the death of Alexander (323 B.C.), his empire was finally carved up into four parts. The Jews were caught between the struggles of the Seleucids of Syria and the Ptolemies of Egypt as they vied for supremacy over Palestine. The latter gained firm control over the region after Ptolemy I, with the help of Seleucus I, defeated the army of Antigonus at Gaza in 312 B.C. For more than a century thereafter Palestine remained under Egypt's rule.

The kings of Egypt appear to have made few changes in administration as practiced by the Persians. Jewish life went on just about the same—at least we hear of no major troubles during the period. Comparative quiet ensued until the accession of Antiochus the Great (223–187 B.C.) to the Seleucid throne. He made a vigorous attempt to wrest Palestine from Egypt but was defeated by Ptolemy IV (221–203 B.C.) at Raphia in 217 B.C. Soon after the latter's death, Antiochus tried again. This time he succeeded. The army of Ptolemy V (203–181 B.C.), a mere child at the time, was cut to pieces in the famous battle of Baniyas, near the source of the Jordan, in 198 B.C.

The Jews, unwittingly involved in these conflicts, received the new ruler with alacrity and demonstrated their enthusiasm by attacking the Egyptian garrison at Jerusalem. In return for their support they received from Antiochus certain welcome considerations—remission of taxes for three years, a general slash of duties amounting to a third of the earlier levy, freedom to practice their customs in accordance with their law, and other privileges. It was for them the sunrise of a new day, once more freed from involvement in internecine warfare between the forces of Syria and Egypt, but Hellenistic clouds, already high on the Syrian horizon, were soon to darken Jewish skies with a density hitherto unknown.

Alexander aimed to weld together the eastern and western worlds by means of a diffusion of Greek culture. In a sense, this ambitious motif was more subtle and far more dangerous for the Jews than the vehicle of political change upon which it rode and which was more superficially apparent to the ordinary man. Alexander's empire disintegrated but Hellenistic culture remained. Greek became the language of the Diaspora Jews, Greek cities sprang up everywhere in the wake of conquest.

In Palestine itself were Sebaste (Samaria), Ptolemais (Accho), Scythopolis (Bethshan), Philadelphia (Ammon), besides Greek trading colonies all along the coast from Antioch in Syria to Gaza near the border of Egypt. Even in their own territory, Jews were not immune from Greek contacts and Greek ways of life and thought.

Consequences of Greek influence may be seen from a perusal of the books of the Maccabees and other Jewish apocryphal writings. New fashions of life were bound to infect Judaism with their novelties. Certain Jews, perhaps of the more "progressive" type, neglected or refused to circumcise their children; the Torah was by many regarded as outmoded, or at best old-fashioned; and the stern morals enjoined by the Law of Moses were subverted by Greek innovations by way of athletic contests, art, and the influx of Greek ideas through commercial contacts and the ability to read Greek literature.

The Abomination of Desolation

The effect of Greek culture upon Palestine Jewry can best be judged from the manifest willingness of many Jews to go along with the new regulations of the Syrian king. There seems to have been no mass resistance, at least at first blush, to the desecrations of Antiochus IV. Following his campaign against Egypt, he subdued Jerusalem, entered the very sanctuary of the Most High, stripped it of its treasures and furniture (I Macc. 1:20–24), and made the city of David into a gigantic fortress. Sometime later he conducted a vigorous propaganda campaign in which he urged the unification of the people around his type of worship.

That he met with some success in this venture is stated specifically: "Many in Israel took delight in his worship and sacrificed to idols and violated the Sabbath" (I Macc. 1:43). But the crowning events of Antiochus' movement were the setting up of the "abomination of desolation" upon the high altar in Jerusalem (I Macc. 1:54; Dan. 11:31; 12:11), the erection of local altars throughout the land, the destruction of all copies of the Torah that could be found and the subsequent wave of persecution of all those who followed the practices enjoined by the Torah. Thus were the Jews, who hoped for peace and the freedom to practice their religion in the wake of the conquests of

Antiochus the Great, betrayed. Those who, in the name of progress, welcomed the new ways and ideas virtually denied the faith and stability of the religion of the fathers.

The decree of Antiochus was more than a mere formal gesture, for he proceeded to enforce it not only in Jerusalem but throughout the land. To that end he sent agents to every village and hamlet with power to compel compliance with the royal edict. To counter the directives of the king two movements arose, one political, the other more or less pietistic in direction. So, when the king's officer appeared at the little town of Modein, some eighteen miles northwest of Jerusalem, the village's chief magistrate, Mattathias, took matters into his own hands and slew both the first Jew who attempted to follow orders and the king's representative (I Macc. 2:15–38). Thus were the fires of rebellion kindled, burning ever more fiercely until the land was purged of paganism a few years later. The course of this struggle, first for religious, then for political freedom, is delineated in I and II Maccabees.

The second countermove against Syrian paganism was inaugurated and carried out by the pietists, the Hasidim. While they joined the Maccabaean family and its supporters at first, their way was basically different. They were concerned primarily about religion and endeavored to promote their cause by way of exhortation to loyalty to the ancestral faith. Matters had progressed too far to right them by recourse to arms. For them there was only one way, the way of God who would intervene, destroy the evil kingdoms of this world and bring in his own. Therefore, it was incumbent on those who trusted in him to remain true, devoted, loyal, for the time of endurance will not be long.

Daniel

Our book of Daniel, as it now stands, and probably also the additions—the Story of Susanna, the Song of the Three Children, Bel and the Dragon, preserved in the Apocrypha of the Old Testament—was composed by a pious Jew in Jerusalem between 167 and 163 B.C. who drew upon the experience of Daniel and his friends to present his views on the rewards of loyalty to the God of the fathers (chs. 1–6). Then in a series of visions granted to Daniel (chs. 7–12), he deals with subsequent history in the Persian, Greek and Seleucid periods with a confident prediction of the impending end of world empires and the joyful consummation for those who remain firm and wait for God.

Chapters 1–6 are viewed as lessons from history, inasmuch as they are couched in the third person singular. Chapter 1 deals with the superiority in appearance and wisdom of the four Jewish youths who refused to defile themselves with the king's food. Chapter 2 portrays the wisdom of Daniel which transcended that of the traditional wise men of Babylon as shown by his ability to recount and interpret the dream of Nebuchadnezzar. Chapter 3 goes a step further and describes the deliverance of the three young men who, by virtue of an unshaken faith in their God, survived the fiery furnace. In both these instances, the Babylonian king is constrained to acknowledge the superiority of the wisdom of the Jews and of the power of their God.

A further example of the wisdom of Daniel and his prophetic powers is given in chapter 4 where he interprets Nebuchadnezzar's dream and predicts a seven-year period of humiliation for the king "until you realize that the Most High has power over the kingdom of men and gives it to whomever he wishes" (4:32 = 4:29 in the Aramaic text). At the end of the specified period his reason returned and he glorified the Most High God. The interpretation of the handwriting on the wall (ch. 5) again reflects the God-given wisdom of the righteous Daniel. Like chapter 3, chapter 6 emphasizes the reward of steadfastness of faith in the Lord who saved Daniel from the mouths of the lions.

The four visions (chs. 7–12) concentrate on the intervening period from the fall of the Chaldean empire to the author's day and are, with the exception of 7:1–2a, related in the first person singular, describing what Daniel saw. There is some difference of opinion as to the identification of the four beasts but they doubtless represent the neo-Babylonian, Median, Persian, and Greek kingdoms with the latter's successors. What Daniel saw was:

> Four great beasts arose out of the sea, different from one another. The first had the appearance of a lion with the wings of an eagle. As I kept looking at it its wings were plucked off and it was lifted up from the earth and made to stand upon two feet just like a man; a human mind was given to it. Then there [appeared] another beast, a second one, in the likeness of a bear. It raised itself up on one side and had three ribs in its mouth, between its teeth; it was commanded, "Arise, devour much flesh." I looked again, and behold, there was another [beast] that looked like a leopard on whose back were four bird wings, and it had four heads; dominion was given to it. Finally I saw in the night visions a fourth beast, dreadful, terrible, and surpassing strong, with large iron teeth. It devoured, crushed and trampled the remainder with its feet. It was different from all the beasts that were before it and it had ten horns. As I observed the horns, behold there came up among them another small horn before which three of the first horns were uprooted, and behold this horn had eyes like those of a man, and a mouth uttering great things.   (7:3–8)

Finally, there will come the Ancient of Days who will assume everlasting dominion over all peoples, nations and tongues after the preceding beasts (kingdoms) shall have been destroyed.

Chapter 8 contains the vision of the ram and he-goat, the former with two horns representing the Medo-Persian empire and the he-goat the king of Greece. In view of the rapidly-moving events to come, Daniel is advised by Gabriel to reinterpret the prophecy of the seventy years of Jeremiah (25:11; 29:10) to mean seventy weeks of years after which doom will overtake the abomination of desolation (ch. 9).

Chapters 10:1–11:39 portray the course of history from the last three kings of Persia to the accession of Antiochus IV, "a despicable one" (11:21), delivered to Daniel in the form of a prophecy. In 11:40–12:3 we have a prophecy predicting the overthrow of the forces of evil and the salvation of the just; not only will the righteous still alive be saved, but "also many of those sleeping in the dusty ground shall awake, some to life everlasting, some to reproach and eternal horror. And those who have acted wisely shall be as bright as the splendor of the firmament, and those who have helped the many to justification (before God) like the stars for ever and ever" (12:2–3).

The concluding verses of chapter 12 (vss. 5–13) offer assurance to Daniel that, though there may be some delay (1290 or even 1335 days), the words of the prophecy will surely come to pass: "Many will keep themselves pure and white and refined; the wicked will keep on doing wickedness—though none of the wicked will understand, those who act wisely will do so" (12:10).

Despite the plethora of problems "in and around the book of

Daniel" and the enigmas present in this and all apocalypses,* it is fraught with tremendous hope and assurance. The times were trying. All sorts of methods of coping with the situation were put forth, but Daniel seems to prefer that of the Psalmist who exhorts Israel to "hope in the Lord" (Ps. 130:7). He would certainly have agreed with the Apostle: "I consider that the sufferings of this present time are not worth comparing with the glory that is to be revealed to us" (Rom. 8:18).

To be sure wickedness and evil have their day but God in his righteousness has the last word.

* Apocalypses are groups of apocryphal writings containing purported visions of things to come and, frequently, predictions of the end of world history.

IN CONCLUSION

From the foregoing chapters it is apparent that the Old Testament is a veritable library of books having to do with man in all his thoughts, relationships and aspirations. All sorts of characters and personalities scamper across the stage of its world theatre. But its chief concern is about man's discovery of God with the fact that he is neither self-sufficient nor wholly mortal.* In other words, God permitted himself to be found of man. There is a side of life today that tends to play down, if not quite altogether ignore, the intangible by whatever name it bears. To the men and women of the Old Testament that was precisely the aspect of life that was most real. They believed in the nearness of God, especially to those who trusted in him and did his will. The Psalmist put it very bluntly:

> Close is Yahweh to those of contrite heart
> (34:18)

> Close is Yahweh to all who call upon him,
> To all who call upon him in sincerity.
> (145:18)

Yahweh was the God of history, which is another way of saying that he was present in every phase of life and experience

---

* See now A. Heschel, *Who Is Man?* (Stanford, California, 1965), p. 119.

from the beginning of creation until the moment when the message and observations of the biblical writers were set down in writing. Each of them were part and parcel of the tradition to which they contributed in their own way as they moved within it and thought about it. The more of time that elapsed and the wider the historical span of the people's existence, the more world history looked like the stage of divine operations always under the control and guidance of the great director himself. He it was in whom all things consisted and converged.

The story to which attention is called in this book is perhaps best epitomized in the words of the author of Psalm 78:

Listen, my people, to my instruction,
    Incline your ear to the words of my mouth!
I will open my mouth in parable,
    I will proclaim riddles from of old.
What we have heard and experienced,
    And our fathers have recounted to us,
We shall not conceal from their children,
    But recount to the coming generation—
The glorious deeds of Yahweh and his power,
    His wonders that he performed.
He set up stipulations in Jacob,
    And gave in Israel instruction,
That he commanded our fathers
    To transmit to their sons.
In order that coming generations may know [them],
    The children [yet] to be born;
That they [too] may uphold them and recount them to their
        children,
    And so place their confidence in God,
And never forget the acts of God;
    That they may keep his commandments
And not be like their fathers,
    A perverse and defiant generation,

An unsteady generation
  That was unfaithful to the Spirit of God.
(The Ephraimites equipped as bowmen,
  Turned back in the time of battle.)
They did not keep the covenant of God,
  And refused to follow his instruction.
They forgot his deeds,
  And the wonders he showed them.
In the presence of their fathers he did wonders,
  In the land of Egypt, in the area of Zoan:
He split the sea and led them across,
  And set up the waters like a dam.
He led them with the cloud by day,
  And all through the night with firelight.
He split rocks in the wilderness,
  And gave [them] drink as from great deeps.
He brought out streams from the rock,
  And made waters flow down like rivers.
But they kept right on sinning against him,
  To rebel against the Most High in the dry country.
They tempted God in their hearts
  By crying for food in their greed.
They spoke against God: they said, "Is God able
  To prepare a table in the wilderness?
Look, he struck the rock,
  And the waters flowed forth,
    Torrents gushed out—
Can he also provide food,
  Or supply meat for his people?"
Therefore, when Yahweh heard it, he became quite angry,
  And a fire was kindled in Jacob
    (Yes, wrath arose in Israel),
Because they did not believe in God,
  Or trust in his salvation.
Then he commanded the clouds overhead,
  And opened the doors of heaven;

He let manna to eat rain upon them,
  And gave them grain from heaven.
Each one ate the bread of the strong,
  Provisions he sent to their satiety.
The east wind he unleashed from heaven,
  And by his power made the south wind blow;
He rained meat like dust upon them,
  And flying birds like the sand by the sea.
He let [it] fall in the midst of the camp,
  All around their dwelling place.
They ate and were fully satisfied;
  What they wanted, he brought to them.
Their appetite was not gratified,
  Even with their food in their mouths.
Then the wrath of God arose against them,
  And he slew [many] of the fattest of them,
    Struck down the young men of Israel.
Despite all this they continued to sin,
  And believed not in his wonders.
Therefore he allowed them to complete their days in vanity,
  And their years in terror.
When he slew them—then they sought him,
  And appealed again to God.
Then they remembered that God was their rock,
  The Most High God their savior.
But they deceived him with their mouth,
  And with their tongue they betrayed him.
Their heart did not remain firm with him,
  And they did not have faith in his covenant.
Yet he was merciful,
  Forgave their iniquity,
    And did not annihilate them;
Often he turned aside his anger,
  And did not arouse his wrath,
For he remembered that they are only flesh,
  A puff of wind passing away irretrievably.

How often they irritated him in the wilderness,
  And grieved him in the steppe!
Again and again they tempted God.
  And caused pain to the Holy One of Israel.
They no longer remembered his hand,
  On the day he delivered them from the enemy,
When in Egypt he performed his signs,
  His wonders in the region of Zoan.
He turned their rivers into blood,
  And the brooks, so that they could not drink;
He sent among them insects that gnawed at them,
  And frogs that devoured them.
The produce of their soil he gave to the pests,
  And the fruit of their labors to the locust.
Their vines he ruined with hail,
  Their sycamores with tornado.
He abandoned their beasts of burden to hail,
  And their cattle to pestilence.
He sent among them the heat of his anger—
  Wrath and indignation and oppression,
    A host of conveyors of evil.
He gave free rein to his anger;
  He did not spare them from death,
    But consigned them to pestilence.
He struck down all the first-born of Egypt,
  The first fruits of their conception of the tents of Ham.
But he led out his people like a flock,
  He directed them in the wilderness like a herd.
He led them safely and they were not afraid;
  The sea covered over their enemies.
He brought them to his holy realm,
  To this mountain procured by his right hand.
He drove out nations before them,
  Allotted to them by measure an inheritance,
    And domiciled Israel's tribes in their [own] tents.

Yet they tempted and provoked God, the Most High,
　And did not hold to his stipulations.
They were as faithless and deceitful as their fathers,
　As treacherous as a slack bow.
They provoked him with their high places,
　And made him jealous with their images.
God heard it and was overcome with wrath,
　And utterly rejected Israel.
He abandoned his dwelling place at Shiloh,
　The tent where he dwelt with men.
He delivered to captivity his strength,
　His splendor into the enemy's hand.
He delivered his people to the sword,
　Because he was very angry with his inheritance.
Fire devoured his young men,
　And his virgins went unlamented.
His priests fell by the sword,
　And their widows could not mourn.
Then the Lord awakened as one out of sleep,
　Like a warrior from a spree,
And repulsed his enemies,
　With everlasting reproach he covered them.
Then he scorned the tent of Joseph,
　And chose not the tribe of Ephraim.
But he chose the tribe of Judah,
　And Mount Zion which he loved.
He built on the heights his sanctuary,
　Like the land which he established forever.
He chose David his servant,
　Took him from the fold of the flock;
From following the ewes he brought him,
　To shepherd in Jacob his people,
　　And in Israel his inheritance.
So he shepherded them with the integrity of his heart,
　And led them with his skilful hands.

That is the word embodied in Jesus Christ who came to fill full the *torah* (instruction) of the Lord and the prophets, the representative of what God meant every Israelite to be. He is not only the Saviour but the pattern of life for all of God's sons.

BIBLIOGRAPHY

The following selected bibliography is intended for those who might desire to pursue further the study of any of the topics discussed. The items starred are especially suitable for laymen.

General

* ALBRIGHT, W. F., *The Biblical Period from Abraham to Ezra*. New York: Harper, 1963.
* ALLEMAN, H. C., *The Old Testament: A Study*. Philadelphia: Muhlenberg, 1935.
* GOTTWALD, N. K., *A Light to the Nations*. New York: Harper, 1959.
* KUHL, C., *The Old Testament: Its Origin and Composition*. Richmond: John Knox, 1961.
* MORIARTY, F. L., *Introducing the Old Testament*. Milwaukee: Bruce, 1960.
  ROBINSON, H. W., *The Old Testament: Its Making and Meaning*. Nashville: Cokesbury, 1937.

Chapter I

* MOWINCKEL, S., *The Old Testament as Word of God*. New York and Nashville: Abingdon, 1959.
* MUILENBURG, J., *The Way of Israel*. New York: Harper, 1961.
  ROBINSON, H. W., *Inspiration and Revelation in the Old Testament*. Oxford: Clarendon, 1946.

SPARKS, H. F. D., *The Old Testament in the Christian Church*. London: SCM, 1944.

* TASKER, R. V. G., *The Old Testament in the New Testament*. London: SCM, 1946.

* WRIGHT, G. E., *The Challenge of Israel's Faith*. University of Chicago, 1944.

Chapter II

* FINEGAN, J., *In the Beginning: A Journey through Genesis*. New York: Harper, 1962.

* HOOKE, S. H., *In the Beginning* (Clarendon Bible Series, VI). Oxford: Clarendon, 1947.

* PARROT, A., *The Flood and Noah's Ark*. New York: Philosophical Library, 1955.

* PARROT, A., *The Tower of Babel*. New York: Philosophical Library, 1955.

* REDLICH, E. B., *The Early Traditions of Genesis* (Colet Library), London: Duckworth, 1950.

* SPEISER, E. A., *Genesis* (The Anchor Bible, 1). New York: Doubleday, 1964.

Chapter III

ALBRIGHT, W. F., "Abraham the Hebrew: A New Archaeological Interpretation," *BASOR* 163, 36–54.

* GORDON, C. H., "Biblical Customs and the Nuzu Tablets," *The Biblical Archaeologist Reader* 2 (New York: Doubleday, 1964), pp. 21–33.

* WOOLLEY, C. L., *Abraham: Recent Discoveries and Hebrew Origins*. London: Faber and Faber, 1936.

Chapter IV

DRIVER, S. R., *The Book of Exodus* (Cambridge Bible for Schools and Colleges). Cambridge University, 1911.

* FINEGAN, J., *Let My People Go*. New York: Harper, 1963.

* NEHER, A., *Moses and the Vocation of the Jewish People*. New York: Harper, 1959.

NOTH, M., *Exodus*. Philadelphia: Westminster, 1962.

* VON RAD, G., *Moses*. New York: Association, 1959.

Chapter V

* ALLEMAN, H. C., "Obedience to the Unenforceable," *Religion in Life* 13 (1943–44), 107–13.

* CHARLES, R. H., *The Decalogue*. Edinburgh: T. and T. Clark, 1923.

MENDENHALL, G. E., *Law and Covenant in Israel and the Ancient Near East*. Pittsburgh: The Biblical Colloquium, 1955.

* POTEAT, E. M., *Mandate to Humanity*. New York and Nashville: Abingdon-Cokesbury, 1953.

Chapter VI

GRAY, G. B., *Sacrifice in the Old Testament*. Oxford, Clarendon, 1925.

* MAYS, J. L., *The Book of Leviticus, The Book of Numbers* (Layman's Bible Commentary, 4). Richmond: John Knox, 1963.

NOTH, M., *Leviticus. A Commentary*. Philadelphia: Westminster, 1965.

Chapter VII

GRAY, G. B., *Numbers* (International Critical Commentary). New York: Scribner, 1903.

Chapters VIII and IX

BURNEY, C. F., *The Book of Judges*. London: Rivington, 1918.

GARSTANG, J., *The Foundations of Bible History: Joshua-Judges*. London: Constable, 1931.

* THATCHER, G. W., *Judges and Ruth* (New Century Bible). New York: Henry Frowde, 1904.

Chapter X and XI

ALBRIGHT, W. F., *Samuel and the Beginnings of the Prophetic Movement.* Cincinnati: Hebrew Union College, 1961.

HERTZBERG, H. W., *I and II Samuel.* Philadelphia: Westminster, 1964.

* KITTEL, R., *Great Men and Movements in Israel.* New York: Macmillan, 1927 (Chapters v and vi).

* WELCH, A. C., *Kings and Prophets of Israel.* London: Lutterworth, 1952 (Chapters 2 and 3).

Chapters XII and XIII

* GRAY, J., *I and II Kings,* Philadelphia: Westminster, 1963.

MONTGOMERY, J. A., *The Books of Kings.* New York: Scribner, 1952.

* MYERS, J. M., "Solomon," *Interpreter's Dictionary of the Bible,* IV. New York and Nashville: Abingdon, 1962 (pp. 399–408).

Chapter XIV

* JAMES, F., *Personalities of the Old Testament.* New York: Scribner, 1939 (Chapter ix).

* KITTEL, R., op. cit. (Chapter vii).

MYERS, J. M., "Elijah and the Yahweh–Baal Conflict," *The Lutheran Church Quarterly* XIX (1946), 393–402.

PEAKE, A. S., "Elijah and Jezebel: The Conflict with the Tyrian Baal," *Bulletin of the John Rylands Library* XI (1927), 296–321.

Chapter XV

* MYERS, J. M., *Hosea-Jonah* (Layman's Bible Commentary, 14). Richmond: John Knox, 1959.

* SMITH, G. A., *The Book of the Twelve Prophets,* I, New York: Doubleday, Doran, 1929.

WELCH, A. C., op. cit. (Chapter v, pp. 130–84).

Chapter XVI

As for Chapter XV.

* ROBINSON, H. W., *Two Hebrew Prophets*. London and Redhill: Lutterworth, 1948.

* SNAITH, N., *Mercy and Sacrifice*. London: SCM, 1953.

Chapter XVII

GRAY, G. B., *Isaiah* (International Critical Commentary), 2d imp. New York: Scribner, 1928.

KISSANE, E. J., *The Book of Isaiah*. 2 vols. Dublin: Browne and Nolan, 1941–43.

* SMITH, G. A., *The Book of Isaiah*, I, rev. ed. New York: Doubleday, Doran, 1927.

* WRIGHT, G. E., *Isaiah* (Layman's Bible Commentary, 11). Richmond: John Knox, 1964.

Chapter XVIII

* GAILEY, J. H., *Micah-Malachi* (Layman's Bible Commentary, 15). Richmond: John Knox, 1962.

SMITH, G. A., op. cit. (Chapter xv).

Chapter XIX

* BRIGHT, J., *Jeremiah* (The Anchor Bible, 21). New York: Doubleday, 1965.

* GORDON, T. C., *The Rebel Prophet*. New York: Harper, 1932.

* KUIST, H. T., *Jeremiah and Lamentations* (Layman's Bible Commentary, 12). Richmond: John Knox, 1960.

PEAKE, A. S., *Jeremiah and Lamentations* (New Century Bible). 2 vols. New York: Henry Frowde, 1910.

SKINNER, J., *Prophecy and Religion: Studies in the Life of Jeremiah*. Cambridge University, 1961.

Chapter XX

COOKE, G. A., *The Book of Ezekiel* (International Critical Commentary). New York: Scribner, 1937.

DAVIDSON, A. B., *The Book of the Prophet Ezekiel* (Cambridge Bible for Schools and Colleges). Cambridge University, 1900.

* SKINNER, J., *The Book of Ezekiel* (Expositor's Bible). New York: Armstrong, 1895.

Chapter XXI

DAVIDSON, A. B., *The Books of Nahum, Habakkuk and Zephaniah* (Cambridge Bible for Schools and Colleges). Cambridge University, 1899.

* GAILEY, J. H., op. cit. (Chapter XVIII).

* PILCHER, C. V., *Three Hebrew Prophets*. London: Religious Tract Society, 1931.

Chapter XXII

KNIGHT, G. A. F., *Deutero-Isaiah: A Theological Commentary on Isaiah 40–55*. New York and Nashville: Abingdon, 1965.

NORTH, C. R., *The Second Isaiah: Introduction, Translation and Commentary to Chapters XL–LV*. Oxford: Clarendon, 1964.

* SMITH, G. A., *The Book of Isaiah*, II.

* WRIGHT, G. E., *Isaiah* (Chapter XVII).

Chapter XXIII

* GAILEY, J. H., op. cit. (Chapter XVIII).

SMITH, G. A., op. cit., II. (Chapter XV).

Chapter XXIV

OESTERLEY, W. O. E., *The Book of Proverbs*. New York: Dutton, 1929.

* SCOTT, R. B. Y., *Proverbs, Ecclesiastes* (The Anchor Bible, 18). New York: Doubleday, 1965.

TOY, C. H., *The Book of Proverbs* (International Critical Commentary). New York: Scribner, 1916.

Chapter XXV

GORDIS, R., *The Book of God and Man: A Study of Job*. University of Chicago, 1965.

* KISSANE, E. J., *The Book of Job*. New York: Sheed and Ward, 1946.

PEAKE, A. S., *Job* (Century Bible). Edinburgh: T. C. and E. C. Jack, 1905.

* POPE, M. H., *Job* (The Anchor Bible, 15). New York: Doubleday, 1965.

RANKIN, O. S., *Israel's Wisdom Literature*. Edinburgh: T. and T. Clark, 1936.

* ROBINSON, T. H., *Job and His Friends*. London: SCM, 1954.

RYLAARSDAM, J. C., *Revelation in Jewish Wisdom Literature*. University of Chicago, 1946.

Chapter XXVI

GORDIS, R., *Koheleth: The Man and His World*. New York: Jewish Theological Seminary, 1951.

Chapter XXVII

KISSANE, E. J., *The Book of Psalms*. Dublin: Browne and Nolan, 1953, 1954.

* RHODES, A. B., *Psalms* (Layman's Bible Commentary, 9). Richmond: John Knox, 1960.

* TERRIEN, S., *The Psalms and Their Meaning for Today*. New York: Bobbs-Merrill, 1951.

WEISER, A., *The Psalms*. Philadelphia: Westminster, 1962.

Chapter XXVIII

GORDIS, R., *The Song of Songs*. New York: Jewish Theological Seminary, 1954.

WATERMAN, L., *The Song of Songs*. Ann Arbor: University of Michigan, 1948.

Chapter XXIX

BATTEN, L. W., *Ezra and Nehemiah* (International Critical Commentary). New York: Scribner, 1913.

BOWMAN, R. A., and GILKEY, C. W., "The Book of Ezra and the Book of Nehemiah," *The Interpreter's Bible*, III. New York and Nashville: Abingdon, 1954.

CURTIS, E. L., and MADSEN, A. L., *The Books of the Chronicles* (International Critical Commentary). New York: Scribner, 1910.

* MYERS, J. M., *I Chronicles* (The Anchor Bible, 12). New York: Doubleday, 1965.

* MYERS, J. M., *II Chronicles* (The Anchor Bible, 13). New York: Doubleday, 1965.

* MYERS, J. M., *Ezra-Nehemiah* (The Anchor Bible, 14). New York: Doubleday, 1965.

WELCH, A. C., *The Work of the Chronicler*. London: British Academy, 1939.

WELCH, A. C., *Post-Exilic Judaism*. Edinburgh and London: Blackwood, 1935.

Chapter XXX

MONTGOMERY, J. A., *Daniel* (International Critical Commentary). New York: Scribner, 1927.

* PORTEOUS, N. W., *Daniel: A Commentary*. Philadelphia: Westminster, 1965.

INDEX OF SCRIPTURE CITATIONS*

GENESIS

1	4, 10, 14 f., 20, 32
2	10, 14 f., 15
3	11 f.
4	12, 16, 17, 44
5	17
6	17, 19
7	19
9	20
10	166
11	23
12–50	24
13	25, 26
21	26
22	166
25	25, 26
31	35
36	166
45	31 f.
47	32

EXODUS

2	34
3	35, 37
6	33
15	36, 181
20	39
22	100
31	57
35	57
36	57
37	57

LEVITICUS

1–10	43, 45, 46, 47
11–15	39, 43
16	43
17–26	3, 39, 43, 54, 95

NUMBERS

1–4	48
10	52
11	51, 52, 53
12	52
13	50
14	50–51
15	47
16	51

* Numbers in first column refer to Chapters of the Bible, in the second to pages of this book.

NUMBERS (cont'd)

17	51
18	98
20	52
21	51, 52
26	23, 49
29	54
36	96

DEUTERONOMY

5	39
6	2, 3
8	3, 56
11	56, 86
14	98
16	54
26	98
32	181

JOSHUA

4	58
5	55, 58
7	106
9	59
10	59
11	59
13–21	23
13	59, 61
19	64
24	59, 86

JUDGES

1	57
2	62, 63
3	63
4	63
5	64, 65, 182
6–9	64

10	64
12	64
13–16	64, 67, 158
17–18	64, 92
19–21	64

I SAMUEL

2–3	68
4	57, 67
7	67, 69
8	67, 70
9–15	70
11	70
15	110
16	73
19	74
21	3, 71
22	71

II SAMUEL

1	182
2	75
5	75
10	76
20	77
22	100

I KINGS

1	79
2	121
3	80
4	80, 159
5	80
6	81 f.
7	81 f.
8	174
9	82
10	82 f.

I KINGS (cont'd)

11 80, 81, 84, 87
12 86, 87, 88, 89, 92
13 92
14 88, 89, 92
18 93, 94, 95
19 95
21 96

II KINGS

7 81
13 98
14 98
15 104, 112
16 110
17 104
19 109
22 122
23 100, 122, 123, 127, 138
24 100, 129
25 130

I CHRONICLES

3 200
6 130
15 207
16 184, 206
18 76
22 206
25 208
26 207
28 206
29 187

II CHRONICLES

2 81
5 206
11 89

12 88, 208
15 206
17 206
19 207
20 207, 208
24 207, 208
26 112, 206
29 206, 207, 208
30 206
34 207
35 123, 206, 208
36 199

EZRA

1 151, 199
2 152
3 152, 153, 200, 206
4 152, 153, 201
7 203, 204
8 207
9 208

NEHEMIAH

1 202
2 203
3 202, 207
4 203
7 207
8 54
9 54, 207, 209
10 209 f.
11 207
13 203

JOB

1 91, 166
2 91
3 166 ff.

JOB (cont'd)

4	170
6	170
8	170
9	170
10	170
11	170
12	170
13	170, 171
14	170
16	172
23	171
31	171
32 – 37	168
38	168 f.
39	168 f.
42	169

PSALMS

3	189
4	16
5	189
8	186
14	9
22	5, 189
24	95, 185
28	189
30	185
31	189
32	187 f.
34	221
42	189
43	189
44	189
45	192
48	185
51	189
70	189 f.
78	67, 222 f.

79	184
90	9
92	185
93	185
96	184
105	184
106	184
113 – 18	185
119	157
130	219
137	130, 145
145	221

PROVERBS

2	160
5	161
6	160, 161
7	161 f.
20	163
23	163
24	160

ECCLESIASTES

1	176, 179
2	179
3	176 f., 178, 179
4	174, 178, 179
5	178, 179
6	178, 179
7	178, 179
8	178, 179
9	178, 179
10	174, 178, 179
11	178, 179
12	174, 178, 179

CANTICLES (Song of Songs)

| 1 | 191, 196 |

CANTICLES (cont'd)
2   195, 196 f.
3   191, 196
4   197
5   196
8   191, 197

ISAIAH

1   113
1 – 39 141
6   91, 112 f.
7   110, 111
10   128
30   111
37   109
40 – 66 141
40   142 f., 144, 145
42   146 f.
49   132, 146 f.
50   147 f.
52   148 f.
53   5, 148 ff., 166

JEREMIAH

2   53, 192
3   192
7   38, 123, 124, 125
11 38
23 91
24 38
25 218
26 123
27 128
29 130, 199, 218
30 38
31 125, 199
32 38, 96, 199
33 199
52 130, 199

EZEKIEL

8   130
10   130, 132
14   130, 165
20   130
26   182
27   182
37   131
40 – 48 205
40   131
43   132
44   132
45   132
47   132

DANIEL

1 – 6   216 f.
6 – 12 216 f., 219
4   216
7   217
11   214
12   214

HOSEA

2   53, 106, 192
4   105, 106
5   106
11 107

AMOS

2   99, 101
3   143
4   98
5   98, 102, 120, 136

MICAH

1   117

MICAH (cont'd)
2   118, 119
3   119
5   115
6   120

NAHUM

1   137
2   137
3   137, 138

HABAKKUK

1   138, 139
2   139

ZEPHANIAH

1   136
3   136

HAGGAI

1   154
2   154

ZECHARIAH

1   154
2   154
6   154
8   154, 155
11   56
13   4
14   54

JUBILEES

34   61

1   MACCABEES

1   214
2   215
7   184

MATTHEW

1   23
2   115
3   23
4   3
7   96
8   155
12   3
19   4
22   4
23   3

MARK

3   47
14   4
15   4

LUKE

1   23, 182
2   182
3   23
4   4
10   4
15   17
16   4
20   106

JOHN

1   13
3   126
6   126

JOHN (*cont'd*)
8   23
15   126

ACTS

1   5
2   5
7   23, 33
8   5
17   5
18   5

ROMANS

1   139
4   23, 28
8   172, 219

GALATIANS

3   28, 139

HEBREWS

9   57
10   139
11   33

JAMES

5   165

REVELATION

18   182
21   133

INDEX

Aaron, 36, 51, 52, 57
Abel, 16, 17, 40
Abiathar, 79, 121
Abimelech, 64
Abner, 75
Abraham, 2, 23–29, 31, 35, 38, 40, 50, 59, 61, 155, 166, 205
Achan, 58
Adam, 2, 17, 20
Adonijah, 79, 121
Ahab, 93, 95
Ahaz, 110, 111
Ahijah, 89, 96
Ai, 58
Ammon, Ammonites, 64, 70, 76, 84, 200, 208
Amon (king), 136
Amos, 97–102, 103, 109, 116, 136, 143
Amram, 33
Anathoth, 79, 121
Antiochus, 212, 213, 214, 215, 218
Aqabah, 56, 82
Arabs, Arabia(ns), 25, 83, 159, 166, 191, 208
Arad, 52
Aram, Aramaean(s), 63, 76, 83, 92, 98, 111, 166, 175

Ararat, 19
Ark, Ark of the Covenant, 57, 58, 67, 69, 75, 92, 93, 112, 120, 207
Artaxerxes, 203, 211, 212
Ashdod, 116
Asherah, 93, 196
Ashurbanipal, 24, 25
Assyria, 82, 98, 104, 110, 116, 128, 136, 137, 138, 152, 201
Azariah (Uzziah), 100, 109, 112

Baal, 67, 93, 94, 95, 96, 106, 107, 124
Baasha, 96
Babel (tower of), 21, 23
Babylon, Babylonian, 10, 19, 127, 128, 129, 130, 132, 139, 144, 151, 152, 153, 166, 182, 199, 200, 201, 204, 205, 216, 217
Bathsheba, 76
Bethel, 13, 58, 92, 99, 100
Bethlehem, 73, 115, 119
Bezalel, 57
Bible, 1, 4, 9, 10, 13, 24, 25, 28, 31, 39, 135, 137, 159, 165, 173, 174, 181, 191

Cain, 16, 17, 40, 44

Caleb, 50

Canaan, Canaanites, 25, 29, 31, 39, 40, 46, 50, 55, 59, 61, 63, 64, 67, 86, 92, 95, 159, 182

Canticles (Song of Songs, Song of Solomon), 191–97

Carmel, 56, 94

Christian, Christianity, 1, 2, 5, 23, 24, 43, 126, 181, 184, 185, 188, 205

Chronicler, 23, 88, 112, 130, 203, 205, 206, 207, 208

Chronicles, 199–210

Council of Yahweh, 91, 143, 145, 147

Covenant, 6, 20, 27, 33, 35, 38, 40, 41, 43, 46, 60, 69, 85, 86, 87, 88, 96, 99, 101, 104, 105, 107, 109, 111, 113, 120, 121–26, 155, 188, 199, 207, 209

Creation, 2, 10, 12, 13, 14, 15, 19, 24, 50, 158, 159, 171, 179, 183, 186, 222

Creator, 9, 15, 35, 159, 186, 187

Cult, Cultus, Cultic, 41, 43, 86, 91, 92, 95, 119, 132, 201, 206, 207, 208

Cyrus II, 144, 151, 152, 153, 199

Damascus, 27, 29, 35, 80, 81, 93, 98, 111, 166

Dan, 13, 64, 92

Daniel, 165, 216–19

Darius, 153, 212

David, Davidic, 2, 13, 57, 61, 68, 71, 73–77, 79, 80, 85, 86,

87, 98, 110, 119, 120, 174, 184, 185, 187, 195, 206, 207, 214, 226

Dead Sea Scrolls (Qumran), 68

Deborah, 63, 65

Decalogue, 39, 105

Deuteronomic, Deuteronomist, 14, 56, 58, 60, 62, 135, 205, 207, 208

Ecclesiastes (Qoheleth), 173–79

Eden, 15

Edom, Edomite(s), 51, 70, 76, 80, 84, 166

Egypt, Egyptian(s), 24, 25, 29, 31, 32, 33, 34, 35, 37, 38, 39, 40, 46, 51, 56, 59, 60, 61, 76, 81, 83, 87, 88, 89, 94, 128, 138, 151, 159, 165, 186, 193, 212, 213, 214, 223, 225

Elath, 82

Eli, 68, 69, 71

Elihu, 168, 171

Elijah, 2, 53, 94, 95, 96, 111, 146

Eliphaz, 170

Elisha, 95

Ephraim, 49, 53, 57, 63, 64, 107, 110, 111, 124, 223, 226

Esau, 26, 27

Esdraelon, 56, 59, 63

Eshcol, 56

Euphrates, 76, 138

Eve, 15, 17

Exile, 199, 200, 205

Exodus, 32, 37, 50, 57

Ezekiel, 127–33, 165, 182, 205

Ezra, 23, 151, 152, 153, 199–210

Faith, Faithful, Faithfulness, 28, 33, 35, 39, 49, 53, 60, 69, 85, 95, 97, 101, 105, 109, 121, 130, 131, 139, 140, 144, 145, 146, 153, 154, 155, 172, 173, 201, 204, 215, 216, 217

Flood, 10, 12, 17, 19, 50

Gath, 117
Gaza, 116, 212, 213
Genesis, 9, 10, 12, 23, 28, 50
Gerar, 82
Gezer, 82
Gibeah, 64, 71
Gibeon, 59
Gilboa, 71, 75
Gilead, 94
Gilgal, 58
Golah, 129, 152, 153, 200

Habakkuk, 128, 138, 139, 146
Hagar, 26
Haggai, 153, 154, 155, 201
Hamath, 98
Haran, 25, 29
Hazor, 82
Hebron, 23, 50, 56, 75
Hezekiah, 109, 111, 206
Hilkiah, 122
Hittite(s), 83, 84, 92
Holy Ghost, 47
Horeb, 53, 95
Hosea, 52, 53, 54, 103–7, 109, 145
Huldah, 122
Hurrian(s), 27
Hyksos, 33

Isaac, 25, 27, 31, 35, 61, 155
Isaiah, 109–14, 116, 141
Ishbaal, 75
Ishmael, 2, 26
Islam, 1
Israel, 31, 32, 36, 37, 38, 39, 43, 45, 46, 47, 49, 50, 52, 53, 55, 57, 58, 59, 60, 61, 63, 65, 67, 70, 71, 73, 74, 75, 76, 80, 81, 84, 85, 87, 88, 93, 94, 95, 96, 97, 98, 99, 101, 103, 104, 105, 106, 107, 110, 111, 115, 117, 125, 130, 131, 135, 146, 147, 150, 156, 157, 159, 160, 165, 173, 182, 183, 184, 205, 206, 207, 214, 222, 225, 226

Jabbok, 53
Jacob, 2, 26, 27, 28, 31, 32, 34, 35, 53, 61, 118, 147, 155, 222, 223, 226
Jehoash, 98
Jehoiachin, 127, 130, 152, 200
Jehoiakim, 127, 138
Jehozadak, 130
Jeremiah, 38, 53, 109, 121–26, 128, 130, 137, 146, 199, 218
Jericho, 50, 55, 58
Jeroboam I, 81, 87, 88, 92, 96
Jeroboam II, 97, 100, 103, 105
Jerusalem, 59, 75, 83, 84, 88, 91, 92, 93, 111, 116, 117, 118, 119, 122, 123, 128, 133, 141, 142, 143, 145, 174, 192, 199, 200, 202, 203,

Jerusalem (cont'd)
    204, 209, 213, 214, 215,
    216
Jesus, 3, 4, 17, 23, 24, 106, 126,
    150, 151, 152, 155, 181,
    227
Jezebel, 53, 93, 94, 95
Joab, 79
Job, 2, 143, 165–72, 173
Jochebed, 33
Jonah, 2
Jonathan, 71, 74
Jordan, 55, 56, 57, 58, 63, 68,
    144
Joseph, 2, 28, 31, 32, 226
Joshua, 50, 58, 59, 60, 61, 62, 85,
    86, 132
Joshua (high priest), 152, 154
Josiah, Josianic, 84, 122, 123, 127,
    136, 138, 206
Jubilees, 61
Judah, 49, 64, 75, 76, 89, 92, 99,
    109, 110, 115, 116, 118,
    119, 123, 124, 127, 128,
    130, 135, 136, 138, 139,
    143, 144, 151, 152, 200,
    202, 204, 205, 209, 226
Judaism, 1, 184, 214
Judges, 61–66, 68

Kingdom: Northern, 13, 118
    Solomonic, 14
    Southern, 79
    United, 13
Knowledge of good and evil, 16
Korah, 51

Laban, 26, 27

Lachish, 58, 116, 117
Lamech, 12
Law, 14, 98
Levites, Levitical, 50, 68, 132, 203,
    205, 206, 207, 208, 209, 210
Leviticus, 43, 44
Lot, 2, 26

Maccabee(s), Maccabaean, 213,
    215
Malachi, 201
Manasseh, 49, 57, 63
Manasseh (king), 136
Megiddo, 63, 82, 88, 123, 127,
    138
Mesopotamia, 24, 25, 27, 56, 63,
    127
Micah, 115–20
Midian, 34, 37, 63
Mishnah, 2, 68, 184, 192
Moab, Moabites, 49, 50, 63, 70,
    76, 84
Moses, 2, 28, 33, 34, 35, 36, 37,
    51, 52, 53, 55, 57, 58, 73,
    85, 96, 146, 184, 209, 214
Mount Nisir, 19
Muhammad, Muslim, 2, 23

Nabonidus, 144
Nabopolassar, 137
Naboth, 94, 95, 96
Nahum, 137
Naphtali, 57
Nathan, 76, 79
Nazarite, 68
Nebo, 55
Nebuchadnezzar II, 127, 128,
    129, 130, 138, 216

Necho, 127, 138
Negeb, 59
Nehemiah, 23, 199–210
New Testament, 1, 5, 6, 7, 23, 141, 182, 184
Nineveh, 24, 25, 137, 138
Noah, 2, 19, 165
Numbers, 49, 50, 52
Nuzi, 26

Og, 52
Old Testament, 1–7, 43, 96, 97, 115, 135, 141, 159, 181, 216, 221
Omri, 93, 95
Ophir, 82

Palestine, 31, 92, 116, 165, 211, 212, 214
Passover, 38, 123, 160, 186
Paul, 5, 23, 28, 35, 38, 172, 219
Pentateuch, 2, 13, 28, 184, 204
Persia, Persians, 144, 151, 152, 175, 194, 200, 202, 211, 212, 216, 217, 218
Peter, 4
Philistine(s), 63, 64, 67, 68, 69, 70, 71, 75, 85, 116
Phoenician(s), 81, 96
Poetry, Poetic, 10, 11, 12
Priests, 45, 76, 79, 94, 120, 122, 125, 127, 128, 130, 132, 157, 160, 199, 202, 203, 205, 206, 207, 208, 209, 210
Prophets, prophetic, 4, 52, 54, 69, 70, 71, 73, 76, 79, 85, 89, 91, 95, 96, 97, 99, 101, 103,
104, 105, 109, 110, 113, 115, 116, 118, 119, 120, 121, 122, 128, 129, 130, 131, 132, 135, 136, 137, 139, 141, 145, 151, 152, 155, 157, 158, 160, 183, 184, 199, 202, 207, 208
Proverbs, 157–64, 175
Psalms, Psalmist, 146, 157, 173, 181–90

Qoheleth, 174, 175, 178, 179. See also Ecclesiastes
Qumran, 175, 182, 184. See also Dead Sea Scrolls
Qur'an, 2, 23

Rachel, 27
Reed Sea, 36, 38, 39, 83, 144
Rehoboam, 86–89
Remnant, 151
Rezon, Rezin, 80, 111
Romans, 38

Sabbath, 40, 160, 185, 203, 209, 214
Sacrifice(s), 43–47, 48, 98, 123, 125, 127, 155, 185, 200, 204, 206
Sale, George, 2
Samaria, 93, 111, 118, 152, 153, 200, 201
Samaritan(s), 152, 153, 200, 201, 208, 211
Samson, 62, 67, 69, 158
Samuel, 67–71, 73, 74, 85, 110, 208

Sanballat, 200, 203
Sarah, 23, 25
Satan, 3
Saul, 2, 69, 70, 73, 74, 79, 86, 110
Sea People, 63
Second Isaiah, 132, 141–50, 151, 155, 166, 199
Sennacherib, 109, 111, 116
Sermon(s), 1, 97, 123, 136, 154, 185
Seth, 17
Shallum, 104
Sharon, 56, 59
Sheba, 77
Sheba, Queen of, 82
Shechem, 59, 60, 61, 64, 86
Sheshbazzar, 152, 200
Shiloh, 57, 64, 67, 68, 75, 85, 124, 226
Shittim, 50, 57
Sihon, 52
Sinai, 27, 32, 34, 37, 38, 49, 50, 57, 65, 105
Solomon, Solomonic, 2, 13, 56, 57, 79–84, 85, 86, 87, 88, 121, 131, 159, 174, 191, 192, 194, 206
Song of Songs, 192, 195
Stephen, 33
Sukkoth, 54
Sumeria, 16
Syria, 25

Tabernacle(s), 186
Talmud, 1
Tekoa, 99, 103
Temple, 81, 82, 88, 91, 112, 122, 123, 124, 131, 132, 153, 155, 160, 182, 200, 201, 203, 205, 206, 208
Tiglath-pileser III, 103, 110, 116
Torah, 2, 45, 49, 101, 109, 123, 125, 126, 139, 146, 151, 183, 206, 214, 227

Ugaritic, 93
Ur, 25, 29
Uzziah. See Azariah

Wilderness, 49–54
Wisdom, 33, 82, 83, 157, 158, 159, 161, 178, 187, 216, 217
Word of the Lord (God), 2, 13, 97, 103, 143, 145, 157

Zadok, 79
Zebulun, 57
Zechariah (king), 103
Zechariah (prophet), 23, 54, 153, 154, 155, 201
Zedekiah, 127, 128, 130
Zephaniah, 135, 136, 137
Zerubbabel, 154, 200
Zophar, 170